MOMENT BY MOMENT

MOMENT BY MOMENT

A Retreat in Everyday Life

Carol Ann Smith, SHCJ   Eugene F. Merz, SJ

Photographs by Don Doll, SJ

ave maria press   Notre Dame, Indiana

Carol Ann Smith, SHCJ

Eugene F. Merz, SJ

Center for Ignatian Spirituality, Marquette University.

Scripture quotations are from the *New Revised Standard Version* of the Bible, copyright © 1993 and 1989 by the Division of Christian Education of the National Council of Churches of Christ in the U. S. A. Used by permission. All rights reserved.

Quotations from *The Spiritual Exercises* taken from *Draw Me Into Your Friendship: A Literal Translation and a Contemporary Reading of The Spiritual Exercises* by David L. Fleming, S.J. Copyright 1996 by The Institute of Jesuit Sources. Used by permission of the publisher.

Photographs © Don Doll, SJ. All rights reserved.

International Standard Book Number: 0-87793-945-4

Cover and text design by Katherine Robinson Coleman

Printed and bound in the United States of America.

Library of Congress Cataloging in Publication Data
Smith, Carol Ann.
Moment by moment : a retreat in everyday life / Carol Ann Smith,
Eugene F. Merz ; photographs by Don Doll.
    p.   cm.
  ISBN 0-87793-945-4 (pbk.)
  1. Spiritual exercises. 2. Catholic Church--Prayer-books and
  devotions--English. I. Merz, Gene. II. Title.
BX2182.2 .S57 2000
248.3--dc21
       00-008684
       CIP

WE DEDICATE THIS BOOK TO

THE MEMBERS OF OUR FAMILIES

WHO GENERATION BY GENERATION

ENRICH OUR LIFE WITH GOD.

CM.

CONTENTS

ACKNOWLEDGMENTS

A book like this would never have seen the light of day without the help of our friends who answered our many questions about the steps involved in taking a text to published form. We are grateful to them and especially to Robert Hamma of Ave Maria Press who gave his sensitive care to our neophyte dream. The Center for Ignatian Spirituality at Marquette University has been our working place and those who gather there with us have made the text a living reality. We are grateful to Don Doll, S.J., and to many others who asked for this book. We hope it finds a place in their lives. Our expression of gratitude would be incomplete without mentioning the Society of the Holy Child Jesus and the Society of Jesus who have faithfully modeled how to live moment by moment in our life with God.

INTRODUCTION

Our lives are given to us moment by moment by a God who is gracious, faithful, and energetically creative in interacting with us. We give our response to God moment by moment in the midst of the ordinary events of our lives. *Moment by Moment* is a guide for reflection and prayer as one makes a daily, particular, life-response to God.

This book came into focus as we reflected upon our experience and our hopes for the women and men working in Jesuit universities in the United States. Simply stated, we hoped that *Moment by Moment* would contribute to their daily efforts to find God in their busy and complex lives. As we developed each of the Moments, we recognized that our book could be of help to any busy person who seeks to integrate faith into daily life. This book offers a way to reflect and sift through one's multiple life experiences and to discover in them the leading thread of God's longing and desire to make us a holy people who are given in service to others.

The structure of the book is reflective of *The Spiritual Exercises of St. Ignatius of Loyola*, a sixteenth-century text containing a variety of prayer experiences intended to occasion a conversion of heart and mind so that a person may follow Jesus with greater faith, love, and freedom. Ignatius first discovered the reality of this conversion experience in his own life and later in the experience of his followers and friends. In light of that, we hope that this small book will also give people already familiar with the Ignatian tradition of spirituality a fresh and prayerful way of entering into the spiritual experience that is at the heart of Ignatian spirituality.

In the past, the Jesuits who carried on the Ignatian tradition have sometimes been described as "the long black line." In our mind's eye, we see a new line, now colorful in its diversity of gender, culture, race, and religious tradition, still moving in a common direction inspired by a common spiritual tradition. The Ignatian tradition—flowing from the unique insight and vision of Ignatius—can only be carried and passed on to others by people grounded in the spirituality of *The Spiritual Exercises*. To remain a living and vital gift to the Christian community, the Ignatian tradition needs to be understood, embraced, integrated, and lived not only by Jesuits, but by Christians everywhere who, in the ordinary circumstances of their lives, strive to give honor and glory to God in this era of human history.

USING THIS BOOK

This book may be used in a variety of ways. It is designed to be used as a retreat made as you go about the ordinary routine of your daily life. This book may also be helpful to people during an extended quiet retreat. It can guide you in a process of regular reflection on your experiences—in your personal prayer, in conversation with another, or in a dialogue with a group. Each Moment may be used for a day, for a week, or for a random hour of reflection when seeking perspective on your life.

Each of you will find your own way of using this book. For some, using all the elements will be helpful, and they will gradually become an unobtrusive focusing structure supporting your experience of God as it unfolds day by day. For others, using just a few elements will provide enough structure to support the *Moment by Moment* experience. For example, any two of the elements within each Moment—the Desire, the Suggestion, the Questions, the Aid to Discernment, the Examen Prayer—used consistently over several months, could serve as a reliable guide for reflection.

It will be up to you to determine how much of each Moment to use as well as the pace of your progress through the book. The key to your choice of how to use it may well be found in that Ignatian notion of using a gift in so far as it allows you to keep your eye on God and your heart open to God's Word. Another of Ignatius' insights will help you to determine your pace: stay with a Moment as long as you find fruit and nourishment there for your relationship with God.

As a help to your prayer, select an environment which will give you some quiet and privacy and which will allow you to be reverent and at home in God's presence. Select a time for prayer when you probably will not be distracted by phones, doorbells, or people. If a quiet place is not available, try to collect yourself into an attitude of quiet and reverence. The photographs may help you to focus your mind and heart as you begin a time of prayer.

Regardless of the way in which you choose to use this book, you will find that you must bring your life experience to it. The consistent format of each Moment will help you to do that. Our hope is that, as you bring your life into dialogue with this book, you will experience at a new level of depth the reality of God's presence with you moment by moment. This is precisely the type of reflection on experience that we see in the life of Ignatius who constantly was searching for God in prayer, spiritual conversation, and service.

We hope that our book will be of help to you as you take the necessary time to step back and ponder the mysterious presence and action of God within your experiences and thus develop a reflective stance. Without reflection we miss the mystery, tend to become weighed down, and see life as a burden. We hope that, by reflecting upon the experiences of your daily life, you will discover how deeply filled with meaning your life is.

THE STRUCTURE OF THIS BOOK

The book is organized in five thematic sections related by their connection to a "Week" of *The Spiritual Exercises*. A **Prelude** introduces each of these groups of Moments and articulates the main themes to be experienced as the subsequent Moments unfold. An accompanying photograph by Don Doll, S.J., offers a visual invitation into the themes to be found in that set of Moments. Taken together, they offer an orientation to the Moments which follow. At the end of each group of Moments, **Replaying the Moments** invites one to open to a deepening of the gifts of the experience. This feature appears at those points in the book when the focus is about to shift (much like the shift from Week to Week in *The Spiritual Exercises*). It reflects the importance which Ignatius placed upon allowing the action of God to penetrate gradually and more deeply into one's whole being.

The Moments are simply constructed to offer a dynamic process through which you may be drawn into the themes and movements of *The Spiritual Exercises of St. Ignatius*. They are designed to engage you in a process of prayer and reflection about your ordinary life rhythms, about scripture and excerpts from *The Spiritual Exercises*. Each moment contains the following elements:

♦ The **Desire** offers an articulation of the grace you seek at each moment. It is meant to guide you as you ask God for what you want and need as you enter into that Moment.

♦ The printed quotations from *The Spiritual Exercises* and **Scripture** are suggestive of the Moment's theme, but surely not exhaustive. Additional scripture references are provided. At times, turning to the full text of the Bible or *The Spiritual Exercises* may be enriching.

♦ Since engaging in some practical action can be a helpful way to dispose yourself for God's grace, the **Suggestion** points to a concrete action which can make the Moment a bit more tangible.

♦ The **Questions** offer a framework for your reflection in the Moment. They intentionally open out in a variety of ways which can further clarify the locus of God's action in your daily life.

♦ The **Aid to Discernment** supports your effort to become more familiar with and sensitive to God's action within you as you move through the Moments.

♦ The **Examen Prayer** is based upon a prayer form within the text of *The Spiritual Exercises*. In the initial Moments, this Examen Prayer unfolds one by one the traditional steps which comprise the Examen. These steps are:

1. Praying for God's light on your experience;
2. Praying in gratitude for God's gifts;
3. Praying about your response to God's action as experienced through the people and events of the day;
4. Praying for God's forgiveness;

5. Praying about people and events which will be part of your life in the next day.

This prayer is usually made at the same time every day, generally at day's end. Once the steps have become a familiar part of your daily prayer, the suggestions for the Examen Prayer are intended to integrate the particular Moment's focus into your reflective prayer about the day just ending.

SHARING THE MOMENTS

Throughout all the years of Christian faith, women and men have talked with each other about their experience of searching for God, of being touched by God, of resisting God's ways, and of walking as loving and loved disciples in the way of Jesus. In speaking to one another, they have expressed in human voice and ordinary details their experience of encountering God. In listening to one another, they have done so enlightened by the wisdom which has resulted from their own years of encountering God.

This simple and profound conversation happened to Mary and Elizabeth; Jesus and John the Baptist; Paul, Peter, and the members of the early church; Ignatius of Loyola and his early companions in the sixteenth century; Cornelia Connelly and her little nascent religious community in the nineteenth century.

That wonderful piece of our faith tradition suggests some possible ways of engaging with others in faith conversation in the twenty-first century. You and your spouse, or you and a friend, may decide to set aside some time each week to share what each of you has experienced as you have prayed during the week. You may want to suggest the use of this book as the focal point of an already established group in your parish or on your campus, or you may want to invite about four or five people to join with you in becoming a group which meets weekly to share the experience of one's reflection and prayer. You may seek out another person whom you know to be a person of faith and wisdom and ask that person to reflect with you on your experience as you pray your way through this book. This person may be your regular spiritual director.

Sharing your experience of *Moment by Moment* with another or with a group will offer an additional Moment within which to notice God's presence and action. A trusting conversation in a simple, reflective manner will allow each person to articulate the experience of a Moment and to respond wisely and with faith to the gifted Moments of others.

◆ ◆ ◆

We are indebted to all the people who have shared their lives with us, deepening our faith and hope that God will be with us moment by moment in this new century and beyond. To them we say thank you. With them, we pray that we may continue to journey together on the road which has brought us to where we are.

PRELUDE 1

"Be still, and know that I am God."

PSALM 46:10

As our lives speed by, they are filled with opportunities to attend more deliberately to the gift of life and to choose to reorient our lives to God in ways which make them more meaningful. *Moment by Moment* begins with reflection on those opportunities.

In the pages which follow, there are suggestions for prayer and reflection which are aimed at helping you to pause in the midst of any busy time in order to be aware of yourself, your desires, your longings.

Our longings and desires, though often expressed in very ordinary ways, are signals to us of our deep desire for God.

Our awareness of God's action and presence to us is heightened by our listening and by our reflecting upon the experience of a given day.

Gradually, one can become aware of those things which block our living a Christian vision of existence and hamper the choices we truly want to make on our life journey.

One learns the wisdom which Ignatius presents in the "Principle and Foundation," the statement giving a fundamental orientation to one's life, gifts, and choices, which appears early in *The Spiritual Exercises*. Ignatius seems to say, "Be clear about this as you set out to live your life for God's glory."

DESIRE

To become more attentive to God's presence and action in my daily routine.

FURTHER RESOURCES

1 Kings 19:4-12

Psalm 37:7

SPIRITUAL EXERCISES

. . . carried on in the face of normal occupations and living conditions . . . truly, it is a retreat in everyday life (Spiritual Exercises 19).

It is good to remember that we are always in the context of prayer. . . . We should always try to maintain a spirit of deep reverence before God . . . (Spiritual Exercises 3).

SCRIPTURE

Listen carefully to me. . . . Seek the Lord while he may be found, call upon him while he is near (Isaiah 55:1-13).

. . . I know the plans I have for you, says the Lord, plans . . . to give you a future with hope. . . . When you search for me, you will find me; if you seek me with all your heart, I will let you find me, says the Lord . . . (Jeremiah 29:11-14).

"Zacchaeus, hurry and come down; for I must stay at your house today." So he hurried down and was happy to welcome him (Luke 19:1-10).

I give thanks to my God always for you because of the grace of God that has been given you in Christ Jesus, for in every way you have been enriched in him, in speech and knowledge of every kind . . . so that you are not lacking in any spiritual gift as you wait for the revealing of our Lord Jesus Christ. He will also strengthen you to the end, so that you may be blameless on the day of our Lord Jesus Christ. God is faithful; by him you were called into the fellowship of his Son, Jesus Christ our Lord (1 Corinthians 1:4-9).

"Speak, Lord, for your servant is listening" (1 Samuel 3:1-11).

QUESTIONS

As I begin to pray and reflect, what desires and hopes do I notice surfacing within me?

What in my life now seems to carry an invitation or challenge to me to become more reflective?

What has led me to use this book and make this Ignatian prayer experience? What do I hope for as a result of this experience?

What people, places, and events in my life have been special instruments of grace in leading me to desire a more intimate relationship with God?

Am I aware of any stumbling blocks that prevent my attentiveness to God's place in my faith journey?

What can I do with the caution I may feel about taking God more seriously in my life?

AID TO DISCERNMENT

As you move through the day, notice the changes of thought, feeling, and mood which occur in you.

We [need to be] aware . . . of our temptations and fears, the consolations and lights given to us by God, and the various movements that happen within us . . . (Spiritual Exercises 17).

SUGGESTION

Begin each day with a brief five-minute conversation with God in which you ask God to bless the hope or desire you have as you begin that day.

EXAMEN PRAYER

At the end of the day, ask for God's light to see how God was present and active in your life that day.

DESIRE

To be more open to the word which God speaks in my daily life.

FURTHER RESOURCES

Deuteronomy 30:11-14

SPIRITUAL EXERCISES

The most important qualities in the person who enters into these exercises are openness, generosity, and courage (Spiritual Exercises 5).

At each stage of the retreat, we need to work as if our whole response to God is found in the material at hand (Spiritual Exercises 11).

SCRIPTURE

O that today you would listen to his voice! Do not harden your hearts . . . (Psalm 95:7-8).

"Listen! I am standing at the door, knocking; if you hear my voice and open the door, I will come in to you and eat with you, and you with me" (Revelation 3:20).

When a great crowd gathered and people from town after town came to him, he said in a parable: "A sower went out to sow his seed; and as he sowed, some fell on the path and was trampled on, and the birds of the air ate it up. Some fell on the rock; and as it grew up, it withered for lack of moisture. Some fell among thorns, and the thorns grew with it and choked it. Some fell into good soil, and when it grew, it produced a hundredfold." As he said this, he called out, "Let anyone with ears to hear listen!" (Luke 8:4-15).

Indeed, the word of God is living and active, sharper than any two-edged sword, piercing until it divides soul from spirit, joints from marrow; it is able to judge the thoughts and intentions of the heart. And before him no creature is hidden, but all are naked and laid bare to the eyes of the one to whom we must render an account (Hebrews 4:12-13).

QUESTIONS

What happens in me when I listen attentively to others?

Reading the psalms can contribute to my reflection, quiet time, and prayer. What do I notice both as I read the psalms and as I reflect on them afterward?

What helps me to recognize the presence and action of God around me? What steps help me to slow down enough to attend to God's presence and action?

When I take a few minutes to quiet my mind and heart and simply listen to my own breathing, what does the miracle of my existence say about God's love for me?

As I try to be open to God's word in my life, what do I notice about the quality of my presence to others?

AID TO DISCERNMENT

The way in which you listen to others gives you clues about the ways in which you listen to God.

For a good relationship to develop . . . and for the greater progress of the retreat, a mutual respect is very necessary. . . . Every good Christian adopts a more positive acceptance of someone's statement rather than a rejection of it out of hand. And so a favorable interpretation . . . should always be given to the other's statement . . . (Spiritual Exercises 22).

SUGGESTION

Each day read a psalm slowly and reflectively. Psalms which you may find helpful are: Psalm 23; Psalm 63; Psalm 103; Psalm 139.

EXAMEN PRAYER

At the end of each day, pray in gratitude for the awareness of God's faithful word spoken to you that day.

DESIRE

To recognize and claim my longing for God.

FURTHER RESOURCES

Psalm 62

Exodus 3:1-6

Exodus 33:12-23

Hosea 6:1-6

SPIRITUAL EXERCISES

The Exercises are, above all, a time for intimate contact between God and the retreatant. . . . For in a retreat we do not find knowledge satisfying us but rather deep down tastes and feelings that sensitize us to what really matters (Spiritual Exercises 2).

SCRIPTURE

"Be still, and know that I am God!" (Psalm 46:10).

O God, you are my God, I seek you, my soul thirsts for you (Psalm 63:1).

A Samaritan woman came to draw water, and Jesus said to her. . . . "Everyone who drinks of this water will be thirsty again, but those who drink of the water that I will give them will never be thirsty. The water that I will give will become in them a spring of water gushing up to eternal life." The woman said to him, "Sir, give me this water, so that I may never be thirsty or have to keep coming here to draw water" (John 4:1-30).

Why do you spend your money for that which is not bread, and your labor for that which does not satisfy? Listen carefully to me, and eat what is good, and delight yourselves in rich food. Incline your ear, and come to me; listen, so that you may live. I will make with you an everlasting covenant, my steadfast, sure love . . . (Isaiah 55:2-3).

O Lord, all my longing is known to you; my sighing is not hidden from you (Psalm 38:9).

Is anything too wonderful for the Lord? (Genesis 18:1-15).

QUESTIONS

What plans and desires in my life demonstrate my longing for God?

What do experiences of incompleteness show me about God as the fulfillment of my life?

What does my longing for God reveal to me about the core of my being?

What do I notice about myself and my thirst for God when I take time to "be still" and listen?

How do I balance my various roles in a consumer society with my longing for God? What habits or addiction can undermine my seeking God?

When my inner well runs dry, how do I respond in faith?

How has my hunger for God's presence been made known to me?

AID TO DISCERNMENT

Notice what happens to your faith and hope when you acknowledge your desire for God.

[Spiritual Consolation may be defined as moments] . . . when we find our life of faith, hope, and love so strengthened and emboldened that the joy of serving God is foremost in our life. More simply said, consolation can be identified with any increase of our faith, our hope, and our love (Spiritual Exercises 316c).

SUGGESTION

Pay attention to the many occasions in a day in which you and others speak of hopes, desires, longings.

EXAMEN PRAYER

At the end of the day, pray in gratitude for being connected to God at the core of your being and life.

MOMENT 4

DESIRE

To grow in my awareness of how I have been loved by God.

FURTHER RESOURCES

Ephesians 1:3-14

Psalm 139

Psalm 104

Psalm 111

Ezekiel 16:1-14

Tobit 8:4-21; 11:16-17; 12:6-22

SPIRITUAL EXERCISES

[Consider] God's gifts to me. God creates me out of love and desires nothing more than a return of love on my part. So much does God love me that even though I turn away and make little response, this Giver of all good gifts continues to be my Savior and Redeemer (Spiritual Exercises 234).

SCRIPTURE

I have loved you with an everlasting love; therefore I have continued my faithfulness to you (Jeremiah 31:3).

Because you are precious in my sight, and honored, and I love you . . . (Isaiah 43:1-7).

It was not because you were more numerous than any other people that the Lord set his heart on you and chose you—for you were the fewest of all peoples. It was because the Lord loved you . . . (Deuteronomy 7:7-11).

For I am convinced that neither death, nor life, nor angels, nor rulers, nor things present, nor things to come, nor powers, nor height, nor depth, nor anything else in all creation, will be able to separate us from the love of God in Christ Jesus our Lord (Romans 8:38-39).

When Israel was a child, I loved him, and out of Egypt I called my son. The more I called them, the more they went from me; they kept sacrificing to the Baals, and offering incense to idols. Yet it was I who taught Ephraim to walk, I took them up in my arms; but they did not know that I healed them. I led them with cords of human kindness, with bands of love. I was to them like those who lift infants to their cheeks. I bent down to them and fed them (Hosea 11:1-4).

22

QUESTIONS

What are my memories of being loved and cared for throughout my life?

What aspect of the created world reminds me of God's care for all humankind?

How have I grown in the awareness that my many talents are God's gifts to me?

When I realize that all that I have and all that I am is linked to God's gifts to me, what begins to happen to my attitudes toward myself and others?

Being loved is an invitation to conversion and transformation. What happens inside me when I try to image a God who is crazy and passionate about me?

How does the gift of being loved by God and others have a spill-over effect on every area of my life?

How have my experiences of loving and being loved allowed me to glimpse God's intimate love and longing for me?

AID TO DISCERNMENT

Notice what happens to your own desire to love as you become more aware of God's lavish care for you.

[Spiritual Consolation may be defined as moments] when we find ourselves so on fire with the love of God that we can freely give ourselves over to God and there is no competition with any human person or any created thing. Rather, we begin to see everything and everyone in the context of God, the Creator and Giver of all good gifts (Spiritual Exercises 316a).

SUGGESTION

As you read the daily newspaper or watch the daily news, notice the diverse ways in which God's love is shown in the world.

EXAMEN PRAYER

After asking for the light of the Spirit, pray in reverence and gratitude for the constant flood of God's gifts upon you and the world.

DESIRE

To grow in the interior freedom needed to orient my life to God.

FURTHER RESOURCES

John 8:12

Luke 8:26-39

Luke 11:9-13

Luke 12:22-34

John 15:1-8

Galatians 5:1

Job 38:1–39:27

Job 42:1-6

Esther 14:1-4, 14

SPIRITUAL EXERCISES

. . . if we are so intent on responding ever better to the love of God wherever it will lead us in our life, we will find the kind of quiet in which the movement of God in our life becomes all the more apparent; our mind will not find itself divided over many cares, but rather its one concern will be to follow the lead of God; in a similar way, our powers of loving, too, will be focused for this period of time solely upon God . . . (Spiritual Exercises 20).

If we feel a disorder in our attachment to a person, to a job or position, to a certain dwelling place, a certain city, country, and so on, we should take it to the Lord and pray insistently to be given the grace to free ourselves from such disorder. What we want above all is the ability to respond freely to God, and all other loves for people, places, and things are held in proper perspective by the light and strength of God's grace (Spiritual Exercises 16).

SCRIPTURE

"If you continue in my word . . . you will know the truth, and the truth will make you free" (John 8:31-32).

As he was setting out on a journey, a man ran up and knelt before him, and asked him, "Good Teacher, what must I do to inherit eternal life?" Jesus said to him, "Why do you call me good? No one is good but God alone. You know the commandments: . . ." He said to him, "Teacher, I have kept all these since my youth." Jesus, looking at him, loved him and said, "You lack one thing; go, sell what you own, and give the money to the poor, and you will have treasure in heaven; then come, follow me." When he heard this, he was shocked and went away grieving, for he had many possessions (Mark 10:17-22).

"For those who want to save their life will lose it, and those who lose their life for my sake will save it. What does it profit them if they gain the whole world, but lose or forfeit themselves?" (Luke 9:24-25).

I . . . beg you to lead a life worthy of the calling to which you have been called, with all humility and gentleness, with patience, bearing with one another in love, making every effort to maintain the unity of the Spirit in the bond of peace (Ephesians 4:1-7).

QUESTIONS

What helps me to grow in gratitude for and stewardship of the gifts I have been given by God?

In what ways do I tend to control my life and treat it as my possession rather than to embrace it freely as God's gift to me?

What signals to me that I am either unfree or losing my freedom in a situation?

In what areas of my life can I be tempted to hold on, to resist change, to act compulsively, or to worry without real cause?

What do I need to do to balance the different aspects of my life?

What people, places, or things need to be given a different priority in order to acknowledge God as the source and end of my life?

AID TO DISCERNMENT

What do you notice about movements within you that signal response or resistance to God's call?

As we begin to be aware of various movements in ourselves . . . it would be helpful to . . . [know] the sources of such movement so that we might be better able to understand how to respond to God (Spiritual Exercises 8).

When we feel tempted to cut short the hour [of prayer], we should recognize the temptation for what it is—the first steps of taking back from God my total gift—and extend the time of prayer for a few minutes beyond the set time (Spiritual Exercises 12).

SUGGESTION

In conversations, notice what you do and what you say when you are feeling unfree or attached to an idea, a project, a person, or an approach to a task.

EXAMEN PRAYER

After asking for the light of the Spirit and praying in gratitude for the many gifts of the day, pray about the response which you gave to God during this day.

DESIRE

To re-order and re-direct all aspects of my life to the praise and service of God.

FURTHER RESOURCES

Luke 12:13-21

Psalm 27

1 Corinthians 12:31-13:13

Psalm 16:1-2, 7-11

Wisdom 13:1-9

Wisdom 7:1-11

Joel 2:26-29

Psalm 150

Psalm 149:1-4

Psalm 138

SPIRITUAL EXERCISES

God who loves us creates us and wants to share life with us forever. Our love response takes shape in our praise and honor and service of the God of our life.

All the things in this world are also created because of God's love and they become a context of gifts, presented to us so that we can know God more easily and make a return of love more readily.

As a result, we show reverence for all the gifts of creation. . . . But if we abuse any . . . or take them as the center of our lives, we break our relationship with God and hinder our growth as loving persons.

. . . we must hold ourselves in balance. . . .

Our only desire and our one choice should be this: I want and I choose what better leads to God's deepening life in me (Spiritual Exercises 23).

SCRIPTURE

For surely I know the plans I have for you, says the Lord, plans for your welfare and not for harm, to give you a future with hope. Then when you call upon me and come and pray to me, I will hear you. When you search for me, you will find me; if you seek me with all your heart, I will let you find me, says the Lord . . . (Jeremiah 29:11-14).

I call heaven and earth to witness against you today that I have set before you life and death, blessings and curses. Choose life so that you and your descendants may live . . . (Deuteronomy 30:19).

Yet whatever gains I had, these I have come to regard as loss because of Christ. More than that, I regard everything as loss because of the surpassing value of knowing Christ Jesus my Lord. For his sake I have suffered the loss of all things, and I regard them as rubbish, in order that I may gain Christ and be found in him . . . (Philippians 3:7-15).

Let the same mind be in you that was in Christ Jesus . . . (Philippians 2:1-13).

QUESTIONS

What attitudes and actions result in my life when I remember the goal of my life is the praise and service of God?

How do prayer and reflection help me to maintain order and priorities in my life?

In what areas of my life do I need to become more indifferent or free enough to want only what God wants for me?

What personal habits of the heart turn me back to God when fatigue or over-extension tend to throw me off balance?

Who or what do I need to surrender in order to entrust my life freely or completely to God?

AID TO DISCERNMENT

Reflect on what you found encouraging (consolation) or discouraging (desolation) during the day.

[Be aware of] the movement of God's grace within . . . so that the light and love of God inflame all possible decisions and resolutions about life situations (Spiritual Exercises 15).

SUGGESTION

At the beginning of each day, look at the items in your schedule for that day and consider how those events will offer you the opportunity to praise and serve God.

EXAMEN PRAYER

Once again, after asking for the light of the Spirit and praying in gratitude for the many gifts of the day, pray about the response which you gave to God during this day.

You now have an opportunity to engage in another moment of prayer. Ignatius calls this review process "repetition." Repetition is grounded in the wisdom of pondering in depth the reality and significance of our prayer experience. From experience and with wisdom, Ignatius encourages us to focus on how we have experienced God's presence and work in the very depth and reality of our own person as well as in contemplating the reality of the world, creation, and Jesus. The use of the repetitions involves the whole person and emphasizes the importance of reflection on experience. It is a holistic approach which, ideally, invites one to accept the truth that an intimate experience of God is possible through prayer. Repetition helps us come to a growing consciousness of God, God's love, God's presence, and God's action.

Replaying the Moments invites you to use the wisdom found in repetition as a way of reviewing and allowing God to deepen the awareness and gifts of a given portion of *Moment by Moment*.

The following questions are meant to guide you in this repetition of Moments 1-6.

As you review the **Desires** of the past days or weeks, what desire continues to capture your attention and hold your interest? Take that desire to the Lord in prayer.

As you look back over this time period, what insight from *The Spiritual Exercises* surprised you with its practical wisdom? Ponder that insight and reflect on how you can incorporate that piece of wisdom into the rhythm of your life.

What **Scripture** passage continues to surface in your consciousness as you reflect on the word of God and your life? What is the Lord saying to you through that passage?

You have seen some practical **Suggestions** presented for your consideration. What suggestions did you find helpful? How are the suggestions helping you to integrate your prayer and ordinary life?

The **Questions** have focused on practical aspects of your life. How have you been helped or challenged by the questions?

During the past days or weeks, several **Aids to Discernment** have been suggested. Where did you find yourself to be most consoled? Prayerfully savor that consolation and allow the experience to deepen within you.

How has the **Examen Prayer** helped you to become more aware of God's presence and action in your life? Reflect on this awareness and allow the Lord to gently deepen it within your consciousness.

What captured your attention in the **Photograph**? How does the photograph support the desires, awarenesses, and insights within your experience of prayer during the last several Moments?

PRELUDE II

"... what mercy the Lord has shown you."

MARK 5:19

It takes only a bit of living to know that life includes more than the experience of being loved and gifted by God. We see that other side of life in the drama of human misery and suffering which flashes across our TV screens and, at times, through our minds and across our hearts. We search for ways to address that painful reality.

With God's help, we can stop denying and avoiding the sight of suffering, evil, need, and sin.

Because of God's mercy and goodness, we are compelled to own our part in that ongoing human drama wherever we live it—in our families, our offices, classrooms, in waiting rooms, boardrooms, on city streets, in any of the many arenas for recreation and investment.

When we are aware of God's mercy and tender care for us, we can even look at the reality of death and allow that reality to help us review the way we are living our individual and communal, societal responses to God.

When we open to the experience of God's forgiving mercy, we are at peace.

Moment by Moment turns now to the astonishing mystery of God's mercy and compassion for us who have so many times joined the group of sinners who ate with Jesus. We are grateful and awed by God's merciful love as shown by Jesus' death on the cross.

Desire

To grow in an awareness of the sin and injustice in our world to which God has responded with mercy and love.

Further Resources

Ezekiel 18:25-32

Romans 8:2-8

Ezekiel 34:1-6

Micah 7:1-10

Spiritual Exercises

I put myself before Jesus Christ our Lord, present before me on the cross. I talk to him about how he creates because he loves and then he is born one like us out of love, so emptying himself as to pass from eternal life to death here in time, even death on a cross. By his response of love for God his Father, he dies for my sins.

I look to myself and ask—just letting the questions penetrate my being:
- *In the past, what response have I made to Christ?*
- *How do I respond to Christ now?*
- *What response should I make to Christ?*

As I look upon Jesus as he hangs upon the cross, I ponder whatever God may bring to my attention. I close with an Our Father (Spiritual Exercises 53).

Scripture

For what can be known about God is plain to them, because God has shown it to them. Ever since the creation of the world his eternal power and divine nature, invisible though they are, have been understood and seen through the things he has made. So they are without excuse; for though they knew God, they did not honor . . . God or give thanks to him, but they became futile in their thinking, and their senseless minds were darkened. Claiming to be wise, they became fools . . . (Romans 1:19-23).

You must understand this . . . people will be lovers of themselves, lovers of money, boasters, arrogant, abusive, disobedient to their parents, ungrateful, unholy, inhuman, implacable, slanderers, profligates, brutes, haters of good, treacherous, reckless, swollen with conceit, lovers of pleasure rather than lovers of God, holding to the outward form of Godliness but denying its power (2 Timothy 3:1-5).

You were dead through the trespasses and sins in which you once lived, following the course of this world. . . . All of us once lived among them in the passions of our flesh, following the desires of flesh and senses, and we were by nature children of wrath, like everyone else (Ephesians 2:1-7).

QUESTIONS

What areas of human misery in the world move my heart?

Which of my gifts do I use to prevent myself from seeing, hearing, or touching human need?

What is evidence to me of the reality of sin and evil in the world?

What do I do with the inner confusion and helplessness that I experience in the face of the systems that seem to deepen the hold of sin on human beings?

In recognizing the social dimensions of sin, what small steps am I willing to take in becoming part of the solution instead of remaining part of the problem?

AID TO DISCERNMENT

Notice the ways in which you avoid making changes that would enhance the quality of life for yourself or others.

When we are caught up in a life of sin or perhaps even if we are closed off from God in only one area of our life, the evil spirit is ordinarily accustomed to propose a slothful complacency in the status quo or to entice to a future of ever greater pleasures still to be grasped. The evil one fills our imagination with all kinds of sensual delights and comforts so that there is no will or desire to change the evil direction of our life (Spiritual Exercises 314).

SUGGESTION

Read beyond the headlines of the story of human suffering in your local newspaper, looking for the deeper causes of it.

EXAMEN PRAYER

After 1) asking for God's light on the experiences of the day, 2) reviewing the gifts you received in the day, and 3) noting your own response to God who has blessed you so providentially, ask God for the light to see how any of your responses are rooted in sin.

MOMENT 8

BLINDED BY SIN

DESIRE

To experience my own blindness, deafness, and insensitivity to sin and evil.

FURTHER RESOURCES

2 Samuel 11:1–12:15

Psalm 130

Luke 18:9-14

Luke 15:11-32

Luke 13:10-17

Mark 10:46-52

Luke 5:17-26

SPIRITUAL EXERCISES

I see myself as a sinner—bound, helpless, alienated—before a loving God and all the love-gifts of creation (Spiritual Exercises 56).

I let the weight of such evil, all stemming from me, be felt throughout my whole being (Spiritual Exercises 57).

I will find that I speak or listen as God's Spirit moves me—sometimes accusing myself as sinner . . . at other times expressing myself as lover or friend. . . . A colloquy . . . happens as I am moved to respond within the setting of the exercise (Spiritual Exercises 54).

SCRIPTURE

Do you imagine, whoever you are, that when you judge those who do such things and yet do them yourself, you will escape the judgment of God? Or do you despise the riches of his kindness and forbearance and patience? Do you not realize that God's kindness is meant to lead you to repentance? (Romans 2:1-11).

As he approached Jericho, a blind man was sitting by the roadside begging. When he heard a crowd going by, he asked what was happening. They told him, "Jesus of Nazareth is passing by." Then he shouted, "Jesus, Son of David, have mercy on me!" (Luke 18:35-43).

For I know that nothing good dwells within me, that is, in my flesh. I can will what is right, but I cannot do it. For I do not do the good I want, but the evil I do not want is what I do. Now if I do what I do not want, it is no longer I that do it, but sin that dwells within me. So I find it to be a law that when I want to do what is good, evil lies close at hand. . . . Wretched man that I am! Who will rescue me from this body of death? Thanks be to God through Jesus Christ our Lord! (Romans 7:18-25).

QUESTIONS

What am I beginning to realize about my own blindness, deafness, and insensitivity?

How has my consciousness of the social dimensions of sin increased with the advent of the Internet?

At home or at work, what are subtle ways I use to ignore or excuse sin, especially any connected to my status or role and its perceived power or influence?

What patterns and dynamics in my life, and in the life of groups to which I belong, can reflect the blindness and foolishness of sin?

What contributes to my being more critical of others' shortcomings and less adept at recognizing my own?

In what way may I be blinded to addictive patterns in my life which inflict harm on myself or others?

AID TO DISCERNMENT

Make efforts to name things accurately, to clarify things which you do not understand, to own your personal responsibility for your actions.

The evil spirit's behavior can also be compared to that of a false lover. One who loves falsely uses another for selfish ends, and so people become like objects at one's disposal or like playthings for entertainments or good times. A false lover usually suggests that the so-called intimacy of the relationship be kept secret because of fear that such duplicity will be made manifest. So does the evil spirit often act in a way to keep temptations secret, and our tactics must be to bring our temptations out into the light of day to someone like our director, confessor, or some other spiritual person (Spiritual Exercises 326).

SUGGESTION

During the day, make choices which limit those things such as noise or exposure to violence which can blunt your sensitivity to both grace and sin.

EXAMEN PRAYER

Continue to conclude the day with prayer for light, gratitude, and mercy. Ask God to help you to respond more faithfully in the coming day.

THE LESSON OF DEATH

DESIRE

To understand death as a reality, as a consequence of sin and teacher of values.

FURTHER RESOURCES

John 11:1-44

1 Corinthians 15:50-58

Luke 16:19-31

Wisdom 3:1-11

SPIRITUAL EXERCISES

I put myself before God and look at the contrast: God, the source of life, and I, a cause of death; God, the source of love, and I, with all my petty jealousies and hatreds; God, from whom all good gifts come, and I, with my selfish attempts to win favor, buy attention, be well thought of, and so on (Spiritual Exercises 59).

I look at my world. Everything cooperates to continue to give me life and strength . . . air and water . . . all the produce of the earth . . . everything contributes to my well-being.

I think of the people who have prayed for me and love me. The whole communion of saints . . . actively works to try to help me.

Everywhere I look, the more astonished I become, seeing so much good coming in on me, while I issue forth so many evils (Spiritual Exercises 60).

SCRIPTURE

Therefore, since we are surrounded by so great a cloud of witnesses, let us also lay aside . . . the sin that clings so closely, and let us run with perseverance the race that is set before us, looking to Jesus . . . who for the sake of the joy that was set before him endured the cross. . . . Consider him who endured such hostility against himself from sinners, so that you may not grow weary or lose heart. In your struggle against sin you have not yet resisted to the point of shedding your blood (Hebrews 12:1-13).

We are . . . always carrying in the body the death of Jesus, so that the life of Jesus may also be made visible in our bodies. For while we live, we are always being given up to death for Jesus' sake, so that the life of Jesus may be made visible in our mortal flesh. So death is at work in us, but life in you. . . . So we do not lose heart. Even though our outer nature is wasting away, our inner nature is being renewed day by day (2 Corinthians 4:7-18).

I consider that the sufferings of this present time are not worth comparing with the glory about to be revealed to us. . . . We know that the whole creation has been groaning in labor pains until now; and not only the creation, but we ourselves, who have the first fruits of the Spirit, groan inwardly while we wait for adoption, the redemption of our bodies. For in hope we were saved. Now hope that is seen is not hope. For who hopes for what is seen? But if we hope for what we do not see, we wait for it with patience (Romans 8:18-25).

QUESTIONS

What are my feelings about my death and the process of dying? What have the deaths of others taught me about living?

What signs of the diminishment of my human powers are evident to me at this time of my life? How am I embracing or resisting those changes?

What are my thoughts and feelings about buyouts, mergers, golden parachutes, early retirement options, the fragility of financial security, nursing homes?

Do negative attitudes or self-defeating behaviors lead me to choose death over life for myself and others, in even small ways? What choices am I making which are leading to death for myself or others?

If I knew I would die tomorrow, what "unfinished business," especially with regard to relationships, would I take care of today?

AID TO DISCERNMENT

Notice the paradoxical way that strength and weakness, power and limitation weave through your daily experience and choices.

The evil spirit can also work like a shrewd army commander, who carefully maps out the tactics of attack at weak points of the defense. The military leader knows that weakness is found in two ways: (a) the weakness of fragility or unpreparedness, and (b) the weakness of complacent strength which is self-sufficient pride. The evil spirit's attacks come against us at both these points of weakness (Spiritual Exercises 327).

SUGGESTION

Prayerfully review your will or durable power of attorney.

EXAMEN PRAYER

As you continue to make the Examen prayer each day, bring into your prayer your growing sensitivity to the fact that choices you make can be death-dealing or life-giving.

MOMENT 10

THE TENDER MERCY OF GOD

DESIRE

To experience God's mercy and love for me as one caught up in the human story of sin.

FURTHER RESOURCES

2 Corinthians 5:20–6:2

Luke 15:11-32

Baruch 5

Romans 8:30-39

SPIRITUAL EXERCISES

How can I respond to a God so good to me and surrounding me with the goodness of holy men and women and the wonderful gifts of creation? All I can do is give thanks, wondering at God's forgiving love, which continues to give me life up to this moment. By responding to God's merciful grace, I want to amend (Spiritual Exercises 61).

SCRIPTURE

Have mercy on me, O God, according to your steadfast love; according to your abundant mercy blot out my transgressions. Wash me thoroughly from my iniquity, and cleanse me from my sin. For I know my transgressions, and my sin is ever before me. . . . Create in me a clean heart, O God, and put a new and right spirit within me. Do not cast me away from your presence, and do not take your holy spirit from me. . . . The sacrifice acceptable to God is a broken spirit; a broken and contrite heart, O God, you will not despise (Psalm 51).

But this I call to mind, and therefore I have hope: The steadfast love of the Lord never ceases, his mercies never come to an end; they are new every morning; great is your faithfulness. "The Lord is my portion," says my soul, "therefore I will hope in him." The Lord is good to those who wait for him, to the soul that seeks him. It is good that one should wait quietly for the salvation of the Lord (Lamentations 3:21-26).

Now all the tax collectors and sinners were coming near to listen to him. . . . So he told them this parable: "Which one of you, having a hundred sheep and losing one of them, does not leave the ninety-nine in the wilderness and go after the one that is lost until he finds it? When he has found it, he lays it on his shoulders and rejoices. And when he comes home, he calls together his friends and neighbors, saying to them, 'Rejoice with me, for I have found my sheep that was lost.' Just so, I tell you, there will be more joy in heaven over one sinner who repents than over ninety-nine righteous persons who need no repentance" (Luke 15:1-7).

QUESTIONS

What events and relationships of my life have carried God's mercy to me?

What are the feelings I associate with being forgiven and treated with mercy?

In what relationships do I need to express God's mercy and forgiveness to others? Is there anyone I need to forgive or from whom I need to ask forgiveness?

How, through God's mercy, have I grown stronger in the broken places of my life?

In reflecting on my weaknesses and strengths, do I recognize them as leaven for God working in and through me as bread for others?

AID TO DISCERNMENT

Allow your feelings of sorrow and repentance to shift your focus from yourself as sinner to God as the prodigal parent who loves you even in your sinfulness.

Spiritual Consolation [may be defined as moments] . . . when we are saddened, even to the point of tears, for our infidelity to God but at the same time thankful to know God as Savior. Such consolation often comes in a deep realization of ourselves as sinner before a loving and compassionate God, or in the face of Jesus's Passion when we see that Jesus loves and entrusts himself to God his Father and to us without limit, or for any other reason which leads us to praise and thank and serve God all the better (Spiritual Exercises 316b).

SUGGESTION

Place a replica of Jesus dying on the cross in your place of prayer.

EXAMEN PRAYER

Include in your Examen Prayer a time in which you praise and thank God for the gifts of God's mercy and forgiveness.

The careful use of repetition allows the person praying to become more open and free before God. Our fine gifts of intellect and memory tend not to dominate in the repetition of contemplations. We are gradually led into the depths of our being and there we can gently rest in God's presence without words . . . heart to heart talk. Through repetition, the word of God can penetrate more deeply into our very being.

The following questions are meant to guide you in the repetition of Moments 7-10.

As you review the **Desires** of the past days or weeks, what desire continues to capture your attention and hold your interest? Take that desire to the Lord in prayer.

As you look back over this time period, what insight from *The Spiritual Exercises* surprised you with its practical wisdom? Ponder that insight and reflect on how you can incorporate that piece of wisdom into the rhythm of your life.

What **Scripture** passage continues to surface in your consciousness as you reflect on the word of God and your life? What is the Lord saying to you through that passage?

You have seen some practical **Suggestions** presented for your consideration. What suggestions did you find helpful? How are the suggestions helping you to integrate your prayer and ordinary life?

The **Questions** have focused on practical aspects of your life. How have you been helped or challenged by the questions?

During the past days or weeks, several **Aids to Discernment** have been suggested. Where did you find yourself to be most consoled? Prayerfully savor that consolation and allow the experience to deepen within you.

How has the **Examen Prayer** helped you to become more aware of God's presence and action in your life? Reflect on this awareness and allow the Lord to deepen it within your consciousness.

What captured your attention in the **Photograph**? How does the photograph support the desires, awarenesses, and insights within your experience of prayer during the last several Moments?

PRELUDE III

"Learn from me."

MATTHEW 11:29

One of the marvels of Christian life is the fact that, as loved sinners made new by God's mercy, we are invited by Jesus to be his disciples.

As we turn our attention to Jesus in the gospels, we seek a deeper knowledge and love of him and his ways.

Ignatius offers a way of praying the gospels that bids us to place ourselves in the scene and to experience the touch of God from within the story. Touched by God, we find ourselves changed. Ignatian Contemplation engages us as whole persons in an encounter with Jesus who teaches us how to serve.

God, in that encounter with Jesus, stirs us with love and transforms our minds, hearts, and choices so that, as the process of conversion unfolds, we become a fuller reflection of Christ for our own time in human history.

MOMENT 11   READY AND ALERT TO ANSWER GOD'S CALL

DESIRE

To hear God's call when it comes and to be willing to respond generously.

FURTHER RESOURCES

Matthew 16:24-26

Matthew 5:3-16

John 8:29

Ephesians 2:4-10, 13-22

SPIRITUAL EXERCISES

. . . I consider Jesus Christ our Lord and his call. If a human leader can have an appeal to us, how much greater is the attraction of the God-Man, Jesus Christ. . . . Jesus's call goes out to all peoples, yet he specially calls each person in a particular and unique way. He makes this kind of appeal: "It is my will to win over the whole world, to overcome evil with good, to turn hatred aside with love, to conquer all the forces of death—whatever obstacles there are that block the sharing of life between God and humankind. Whoever wishes to join me in this mission must be willing to labor with me, and so by following me in struggle and suffering may share with me in glory" (Spiritual Exercises 95).

SCRIPTURE

"What do you think? A man had two sons; he went to the first and said, 'Son, go and work in the vineyard today.' He answered, 'I will not'; but later he changed his mind and went. The father went to the second and said the same; and he answered, 'I go, sir'; but he did not go. Which of the two did the will of his father?" They said, "The first." Jesus said to them, "Truly I tell you, the tax collectors and the prostitutes are going into the kingdom of God ahead of you" (Matthew 21:28-32).

". . . But if God so clothes the grass of the field, which is alive today and tomorrow is thrown into the oven, how much more will he clothe you—you of little faith! And do not keep striving for what you are to eat and what you are to drink, and do not keep worrying. . . . Your Father knows that you need them. Instead, strive for his kingdom, and these things will be given to you as well" (Luke 12:22-31).

Jesus said to them, "My food is to do the will of him who sent me and to complete his work" (John 4:34).

QUESTIONS

What role have heroes and heroines played in my life? Who have been the mentors and models whose lives and values have inspired me?

What dreams, values, and issues stir my passionate concern at this time in my life?

What is there about the person and priorities of Jesus which has drawn me into being a Christian disciple?

What in my life symbolizes my willingness to commit my energies to the person and values of Jesus?

Regardless of my age or other life circumstances, what freedom is there in my life for dreaming and imagining how to extend the reign of God?

How am I concretely making efforts at correcting unjust actions, decisions, and systems?

In all honesty, what do I hesitate to give up or to do in order to better respond to God's call?

AID TO DISCERNMENT

At this point in the retreat, notice how your chosen place and rhythm of prayer are supporting your growing attentiveness to God's action within you. Make any adjustments which will help you to be more sensitive to God's invitation during prayer and throughout the day.

I take the usual time to place myself before God in reverence, begging that everything in my day be more and more directed to God's service and praise (Spiritual Exercises 91).

SUGGESTION

Recall what you know of the story of Ignatius of Loyola and his passionate desire to serve Christ.

EXAMEN PRAYER

In your prayer, include gratitude for the people who have inspired you to give yourself generously in Christ's service.

"THE WORD WAS MADE FLESH AND DWELT AMONG US"

DESIRE

To deepen my faith and trust in God who has become human in Jesus.

SPIRITUAL EXERCISES

I try to enter into the vision of God—the mystery of divinity shared by three divine persons—looking upon our world: men and women being born and being laid to rest, some getting married and others getting divorced, the old and the young, the rich and the poor, the happy and the sad, so many people aimless, despairing, hateful and killing, so many undernourished, sick, and dying, so many struggling with life and blind to any meaning. With God, I can hear people laughing and crying, some shouting and screaming, some praying, others cursing.

The leap of divine joy: God knows the time has come when the mystery of salvation, hidden from the beginning of the world, will shine into human darkness and confusion. It is as if I can hear the Divine Persons saying, "Let us work the redemption of the whole human race; let us respond to the groaning of all creation" (Spiritual Exercises 102, 103, 106, 107).

FURTHER RESOURCES

Wisdom 18:14-15

Isaiah 9:1-6

Titus 3:4-7

SCRIPTURE

The angel said, "Do not be afraid, Mary, for you have found favor with God. You will conceive in your womb and bear a son, and you will name him Jesus. . . ." Mary said "How can this be, since I am a virgin?" The angel said "The Holy Spirit will come upon you, the power of the Most High will overshadow you; therefore the child to be born will be holy; he will be called Son of God. . . ." Mary said, "Here am I, the servant of the Lord; let it be with me according to your word" (Luke 1:26-38)

In the beginning was the Word, and the Word was with God, and the Word was God. . . . All things came into being through him, and without him not one thing came into being. What has come into being in him was life, and the life was the light of all people. . . . And the Word became flesh and lived among us, and we have seen his glory. . . . From his fullness we have all received, grace upon grace . . . (John 1:1-18).

QUESTIONS

What aspects of being human are delightful to me? What aspects can be burdensome?

What daily choices foster my respect for the humanity of others?

What are my deepest desires for my own humanity? What do I long for to help me to become more authentically human?

In what areas of my life am I being asked to say "yes" to God as Mary did?

What do I do with my questions about the ways in which God seems to work in my life?

How do I respond through the use of my gifts and talents to the "groaning of all creation"?

From God's goodness, I have received "grace upon grace." Which ones surface for me at this moment and what might be the significance of that awareness or memory?

AID TO DISCERNMENT

Give particular attention to how God may be speaking to you in your own humanity, e.g., through your energy level, your sexuality, your attention span, your methods of working and relaxing, the general condition of your health.

I let myself be totally present to the scene, hearing the nuances of the questions, seeing the expression in the face and eyes, watching the gestures and movements which tell us so much about a person.

I notice how our triune God works—so simply and quietly, so patiently. A world goes on, apparently oblivious to the new creation which has begun. I take in Mary's complete way of being available and responding to her Lord and God (Spiritual Exercises 108).

SUGGESTION

While at a shopping mall, supermarket, reception, sports event, etc., take five or ten minutes to gaze upon the people with reverence for our shared humanity in all its diversity.

EXAMEN PRAYER

Allow your gratitude to deepen for the gifts of God which you experience in other human beings and in your own humanity.

MOMENT 13

"GOD SO LOVED THE WORLD . . ."

DESIRE

To deepen my love of and commitment to Jesus who in becoming human has embraced weakness.

FURTHER RESOURCES

1 John 1:1-4

1 John 3:1-3

Hebrews 2:14-18

Hebrews 1:1-6

SPIRITUAL EXERCISES

As I find myself immersed in the setting of this mystery of the Incarnation, I may want just to stay with Mary or with the eternal Word, who has now become human—for me. Sometimes I may want to speak out my joy, my thanks, my wonder, or my praise to the three Divine Persons. According to the light of God's grace given to me, I beg that I might come to know Jesus as a pattern for my own living and so be able to draw close to him (Spiritual Exercises 109).

SCRIPTURE

[Joseph] went to be registered with Mary, to whom he was engaged and who was expecting a child. While they were there, the time came for her to deliver her child. And she gave birth to her firstborn son and wrapped him in bands of cloth, and laid him in a manger, because there was no place for them in the inn. In that region there were shepherds living in the fields, keeping watch over their flock by night. . . . But the angel said to them, "Do not be afraid; for see—I am bringing you good news of great joy for all the people: to you is born this day in the city of David a Savior, who is the Messiah, the Lord. This will be a sign for you: you will find a child wrapped in bands of cloth and lying in a manger" (Luke 2:1-14).

Now there was a man in Jerusalem whose name was Simeon; this man was righteous and devout, looking forward to the consolation of Israel, and the Holy Spirit rested on him. It had been revealed to him by the Holy Spirit that he would not see death before he had seen the Lord's Messiah. Guided by the Spirit, Simeon . . . took [the child Jesus] in his arms and praised God, saying, "Master, now you are dismissing your servant in peace, according to your word; for my eyes have seen your salvation. . . ." There was also a prophet, Anna. . . . She was of a great age, having lived with her husband seven years after her marriage, then as a widow to the age of eighty-four. She never left the temple but worshiped there with fasting and prayer night and day. At that moment she came, and began to praise God and to speak about the child to all who were looking for the redemption of Jerusalem. When [the parents] had finished everything required by the law of the Lord, they returned to Galilee, to their own town of Nazareth. The child grew and became strong, filled with wisdom; and the favor of God was upon him (Luke 2:22-40).

QUESTIONS

How do I feel around very young children or very old adults?

How is my work contributing to the well-being of people who are fragile in any way, e.g., the elderly, the mentally or emotionally ill, children, immigrants?

How do I respond in moments of vulnerability and powerlessness?

How am I challenged in my life and work in contemporary culture by what I see as God's choice of poverty and powerlessness in the birth of Jesus?

Do I allow the remembrance of the birth of Jesus to deepen my love for Jesus who shares my humanity?

In what ways do I want to know Jesus as a pattern for my own living?

Who and what has taught me to be gentle with myself and with others? How is my life linked to caring for people?

AID TO DISCERNMENT

Notice the quality of peace which you experience when you are "at home" in your humanity.

Perhaps there is little to say because this style of contemplation is often more a "being with" experience than a word-response (Spiritual Exercises 117).

A deep-down peace comes in just our living life as "being in our Father's house" (Spiritual Exercises 316c).

SUGGESTION

Review the physical conditions of your neighborhood, institution, business, parish, and home to see how helpful they are to people with physical disabilities.

EXAMEN PRAYER

As you review your response to God's gifts to you in a day, be alert to any harshness to the human which has been part of your response.

MOMENT 14 THE ORDINARY DAYS IN LIFE

DESIRE

To deepen my love for Jesus and his way of living the ordinary days of his life.

FURTHER RESOURCES

1 John 3:18

1 Peter 3:8-9; 4:8-11

James 1:2-6, 19, 22-25

Hebrews 1:1-3a

Colossians 3:12-21

Ephesians 1:3-6, 15-18

SPIRITUAL EXERCISES

One way of considering the mysteries of Jesus's early life is to see the interpretative direction in which they point. The ordinary life of the Christian is exemplified in Christ's obedience to his parents in the ordinary life of Nazareth. But the call to service in the Father's house is already manifested in the mystery of Jesus's remaining in the temple at the age of twelve to the consternation of his mother and father.

While I continue to contemplate Jesus's life, let me begin to examine myself and ask to what state of life or to what style of living is our loving, provident God leading me (Spiritual Exercises 135).

SCRIPTURE

When they had finished everything required by the law of the Lord, they returned to Galilee, to their own town of Nazareth. The child grew and became strong, filled with wisdom; and the favor of God was upon him. . . . After three days they found him in the temple, sitting among the teachers, listening to them and asking them questions. And all who heard him were amazed at his understanding and his answers. When his parents saw him they were astonished; and his mother said to him, "Child, why have you treated us like this? Look, your father and I have been searching for you in great anxiety." He said to them, "Why were you searching for me? Did you not know that I must be in my Father's house?" But they did not understand what he said to them. Then he went down with them and came to Nazareth, and was obedient to them. His mother treasured all these things in her heart. And Jesus increased in wisdom and in years, and in divine and human favor (Luke 2:39-52).

Beloved, since God loved us so much, we also ought to love one another. No one has ever seen God; if we love one another, God lives in us, and his love is perfected in us (1 John 4:7-19).

Rejoice in the Lord always; again I will say, Rejoice. Let your gentleness be known to everyone.

The Lord is near. Do not worry about anything, but in everything by prayer and supplication with thanksgiving let your requests be made known to God. And the peace of God, which surpasses all understanding, will guard your hearts and your minds in Christ Jesus. (Philippians 4:4-9).

QUESTIONS

Which of my daily activities do I consider "ordinary"?

How does my awareness of God's presence and action during ordinary activities alter my judgment about their importance?

In my life now, who are the people whose ordinary work enhances the quality of my life?

What practical humility is required of me in the often hidden work I do? How can I develop that attitude so it is more like the humility of Jesus?

What have I learned about myself in moments of receiving praise, affirmation, congratulations, or a prize? What helps me to be grateful to God at those times? How are they serving to deepen my relationship with God?

Jesus was born poor and raised in impoverished circumstances. What effect does this reality have on the lifestyle choices I make?

AID TO DISCERNMENT

Notice whether you experience consolation or desolation in the midst of your ordinary daily activity.

A time of consolation should provide the opportunity for a growth in true humility. We can acknowledge with gratitude the gifts we have received and recognize the full gratuity of God's favor. It may be well to take stock how poorly we fare when such consolation is withdrawn. On the other hand, if we are afflicted by desolation, we should take some consolation in knowing that God's grace is always sufficient to follow the way of the Lord (Spiritual Exercises 324).

SUGGESTION

Begin one of your ordinary tasks with a brief prayer to Jesus, the apprentice of Joseph the Carpenter.

EXAMEN PRAYER

In your opening prayer for God's light, ask God to show you how to focus on God's action in the day more than on your own.

MOMENT 15

MY IDENTITY IN CHRIST

DESIRE

To appreciate more fully the identity of Jesus as God's beloved Son.

FURTHER RESOURCES

Ephesians 2:8-10

Ephesians 4:1-7, 11-16

Philippians 3:12-16

Colossians 3:1-4, 12-17

Isaiah 42: 1-4, 6-7

SPIRITUAL EXERCISES

When we are trying to follow the loving invitation of God in our life, we will find that the good spirit tends to give support, encouragement, and oftentimes even a certain delight in all our endeavors. The evil spirit generally acts to bring about the opposite reaction.

The evil spirit will subtly arouse a dissatisfaction with our own efforts, will raise up doubts and anxieties about God's love or our own response, or will upset our conscience by suggesting thoughts of pride in our attempt to lead a good life (Spiritual Exercises 329).

SCRIPTURE

Then Jesus came from Galilee to John at the Jordan, to be baptized by him. . . . And when Jesus had been baptized, just as he came up from the water, suddenly the heavens were opened to him and he saw the Spirit of God descending like a dove and alighting on him. And a voice from heaven said, "This is my Son, the Beloved, with whom I am well pleased" (Matthew 3:13-17).

Since, then, we have a great high priest who has passed through the heavens, Jesus, the Son of God, let us hold fast to our confession. For we do not have a high priest who is unable to sympathize with our weaknesses, but we have one who in every respect has been tested as we are, yet without sin. Let us therefore approach the throne of grace with boldness, so that we may receive mercy and find grace to help in time of need (Hebrews 4:14-16).

As you therefore have received Christ Jesus the Lord, continue to live your lives in him, rooted and built up in him and established in the faith, just as you were taught, abounding in thanksgiving (Colossians 2:6-8).

QUESTIONS

How do I identify myself when I am meeting people for the first time? What does that tell me about how I view myself?

How has my self-understanding changed since I was eighteen? What has matured me?

What does my baptismal identity mean to me? What difference does it make in my choices?

How do I experience temptations to ignore or compromise my personal and Christian identity? What has been the fruit of my struggles to live in a way that is true to my identity?

What helps me to integrate my various roles into my basic identity?

In what ways do I consider what I do and accomplish as being more important than who I am before God?

AID TO DISCERNMENT

As you sign your name or give it to others in conversation, do so with an intention to embrace your identity with acceptance and humility.

When we find ourselves weighted down by a certain desolation, we should not try to change a previous decision or to come to a new decision. The reason is that in desolation the evil spirit is making an attempt to obstruct the good direction of our life or to change it, and so we would be thwarted from the gentle lead of God and what is more conducive to our own salvation. As a result, at a time of desolation, we hold fast to the decision which guided us during the time before the desolation came on us (Spiritual Exercises 318).

SUGGESTION

Reflect on the significance for your identity of the name you were given and the titles you may have.

EXAMEN PRAYER

As you review God's gifts to you and your response, notice how they are helping to shape your personal and Christian identity.

DESIRE

To experience the call of God to be a disciple who loves Jesus intimately and follows him closely.

FURTHER RESOURCES

1 Corinthians 1:4-9

Ephesians 1:15-19

SPIRITUAL EXERCISES

With God inviting and with victory assured, how can anyone in their right mind not surrender to Jesus and his call to labor with him? (Spiritual Exercises 96).

SCRIPTURE

Jesus was standing beside the lake of Gennesaret, and the crowd was pressing in on him to hear the word of God, he saw two boats there at the shore of the lake; the fishermen had gone out of them and were washing their nets. He got into one of the boats, the one belonging to Simon, and asked him to put out a little way from the shore. Then he sat down and taught the crowds from the boat. When he had finished speaking, he said to Simon, "Put out into the deep water and let down your nets for a catch." Simon answered, "Master, we have worked all night long but have caught nothing. Yet if you say so, I will let down the nets." When they had done this, they caught so many fish that their nets were beginning to break. So they signaled their partners in the other boat to come and help them. And they came and filled both boats, so that they began to sink. But when Simon Peter saw it, he fell down at Jesus' knees, saying, "Go away from me, Lord, for I am a sinful man!". . . Then Jesus said to Simon, "Do not be afraid; from now on you will be catching people." When they had brought their boats to shore, they left everything and followed him (Luke 5:1-11).

Now there are varieties of gifts, but the same Spirit; and there are varieties of services, but the same Lord; and there are varieties of activities, but it is the same God who activates all of them in everyone. To each is given the manifestation of the Spirit for the common good (1 Corinthians 12:4-7).

And immediately they left their nets and followed him (Mark 1:16-20).

QUESTIONS

When have I known or experienced God's invitation or call?

What have the relationships in my life taught me about commitment and the renewed choices it requires?

In the key relationships active now in my life, how am I being asked to be more like the person of Jesus?

What has been costly to me in my efforts to be a reliable and responsible spouse, child, friend, colleague, alumna/alumnus, administrator, professor, neighbor, employee, citizen?

What have been the moments of intimacy with Jesus in my life? In what circumstances have they occurred? Do I consider Jesus an intimate friend?

What do I learn by reflecting on those times in my life when I have experienced full as well as empty nets?

In what ways do I acknowledge my God-given gifts and talents and humbly, generously, offer them back in service to God's people?

Do I encourage and mentor others by revealing their own, often hidden, gifts to them?

AID TO DISCERNMENT

Look through an address book or an assortment of personal photographs to help you ponder the fact that the loving intimate relationships of our lives are often the places where we experience the call of Christ to follow him more closely.

Colloquy: As I find myself immersed in the . . . mystery of the Incarnation, I may want just to stay with Mary or with the eternal Word, who has . . . become human—for me. Sometimes I may want to speak out my joy, my thanks, my wonder, or my praise. . . . According to . . . God's grace given to me, I beg that I might come to know Jesus as a pattern for my own living and so be able to draw close to him (Spiritual Exercises 109).

SUGGESTION

Read the Gospel of Mark to refresh your memory about the person and mission of Jesus.

EXAMEN PRAYER

As you ask for God's help in the coming day, ask for a deeper fidelity in the relationships of your life.

DESIRE

In wonder and awe, to contemplate Jesus, whose human life reveals the heart of God.

FURTHER RESOURCES

Luke 7:36-50

John 2:1-12

Philippians 2:1-13

John 2:13-25

Mark 9:14-29

SPIRITUAL EXERCISES

I ask for the grace to know Jesus intimately, to love him more intensely, and so to follow him more closely (Spiritual Exercises 104).

SCRIPTURE

He came to his hometown and began to teach the people in their synagogue, so that they were astounded and said, "Where did this man get this wisdom and these deeds of power? Is not this the carpenter's son? Is not his mother called Mary? And are not his brothers James and Joseph and Simon and Judas? And are not all his sisters with us? Where then did this man get all this?" (Matthew 13:54-58).

They brought to him a deaf man who had an impediment in his speech; and they begged him to lay his hand on him. He took him aside in private, away from the crowd, and put his fingers into his ears, and he spat and touched his tongue. Then looking up to heaven, he sighed and said to him, "Ephphatha," that is, "Be opened." And immediately his ears were opened, his tongue was released, and he spoke plainly. Then Jesus ordered them to tell no one; but the more he ordered them, the more zealously they proclaimed it. They were astounded beyond measure, saying, "He has done everything well; he even makes the deaf to hear and the mute to speak" (Mark 7:31-37).

Jesus went on with his disciples to the villages of Caesarea Philippi; and on the way he asked his disciples, "Who do people say that I am?" And they answered him, "John the Baptist; and others, Elijah; and still others, one of the prophets." He asked them, "But who do you say that I am?" Peter answered him, "You are the Messiah" (Mark 8:27-29).

QUESTIONS

What events in the public life of Jesus draw me to him?

What is there about Jesus which evokes a response of faith and trust from me?

As I reflect on the life of Jesus, what attracts or draws me to spend time with him?

What part of the message of Jesus is challenging to me at this time in my life?

From looking at Jesus, what do I discover about reverencing other people?

Jesus frequently associated with marginalized people. Am I comfortable with marginalized friends of Jesus in our world?

As I reflect on how Jesus treated others, particularly the outcasts of society, in what ways do I want to be empowered by Jesus to live the call of the gospels more fully?

AID TO DISCERNMENT

Notice the desire to be generous which stirs in you when you read the following prayer.

Lord, teach me to be generous. Teach me to serve You as You deserve; to give and not to count the cost; to fight and not to heed the wounds; to toil and not to seek for rest; to labor and not ask for reward, save that of knowing that I am doing Your will.

—"Prayer of Generosity," St. Ignatius of Loyola

SUGGESTION

Consider the images of Jesus or moments in his life which have been important to you at different times in your life.

EXAMEN PRAYER

Address your prayer for help in the upcoming day to the person of Jesus.

DESIRE

To reverence the unique invitations of God which have given shape and form to my life and decisions.

FURTHER RESOURCES

John 3:1-21

Isaiah 42:5-9

John 4:1-15

Luke 10:38-42

1 John 3:1-3, 16-18

Luke 7:18-23

SPIRITUAL EXERCISES

Those who are of great heart and set on fire with zeal to follow Jesus . . . will not only offer themselves entirely to labor for such a mission, but will act against anything which would make their response less total (Spiritual Exercises 97).

SCRIPTURE

Now the word of the Lord came to me saying, "Before I formed you in the womb I knew you, and before you were born I consecrated you; I appointed you a prophet to the nations." Then I said, "Ah, Lord God! Truly I do not know how to speak, for I am only a boy." But the Lord said to me, "Do not say, 'I am only a boy'; for you shall go to all to whom I send you, and you shall speak whatever I command you. Do not be afraid of them, for I am with you to deliver you," says the Lord (Jeremiah 1:4-8).

I want to know Christ and the power of his resurrection and the sharing of his sufferings by becoming like him in his death, if somehow I may attain the resurrection from the dead. Not that I have already obtained this or have already reached the goal; but I press on to make it my own, because Christ Jesus has made me his own. Beloved, I do not consider that I have made it my own; but this one thing I do: forgetting what lies behind and straining forward to what lies ahead, I press on toward the goal for the prize of the heavenly call of God in Christ Jesus (Philippians 3:7-14).

For this reason, since the day we heard it, we have not ceased praying for you and asking that you may be filled with the knowledge of God's will in all spiritual wisdom and understanding, so that you may lead lives worthy of the Lord, fully pleasing to him, as you bear fruit in every good work and as you grow in the knowledge of God. May you be made strong with all the strength that comes from his glorious power, and may you be prepared to endure everything with patience, while joyfully giving thanks to the Father, who has enabled you to share in the inheritence of the saints in the light (Colossians 1:9-12).

QUESTIONS

What does my personal history reveal to me of the particular ways in which I have been called by God?

What role has my family of origin played in my personal vocation?

What place have my gifts of mind, body, personality, and spirit had in my response to God's call?

How does my understanding of the meaning of my life change when I view it in terms of a personal vocation?

How does my personal vocation reveal to me the way in which I am meant to be a disciple?

Jesus celebrated and wept with friends. What have my close friendships revealed to me about the heart of God?

AID TO DISCERNMENT

Notice what happens within you when you make choices to live in harmony with your personal vocation.

The good spirit, however, strengthens and encourages, consoles and inspires, establishes a peace and sometimes moves to a firm resolve. To lead a good life gives delight and joy, and no obstacle seems to be so formidable that it cannot be faced and overcome with God's grace. The good spirit thereby continues an upright person's progress in responding to God's continuing invitation (Spiritual Exercises 315).

We grow into this freedom by gradually bringing an order of values into our lives so that we find that at the moment of choice or decision we are not swayed by any disordered love (Spiritual Exercises 21).

SUGGESTION

Do a simple time line of your own life, noting events and people which, in God's providence, have been a significant part of your entire life.

EXAMEN PRAYER

Focus your gratitude upon the events which show God's faithful and provident call to you.

59

DESIRE

To recognize the ways in which God's light and the darkness of evil can both attract me and influence my choices.

FURTHER RESOURCES

Matthew 11:28-30

1 Peter 5:8-11

Luke 9:28-36

Galatians 5:16-26

Hebrews 4:14-16

John 10:1-18

Ephesians 6:10-20

Mark 10:17-27

Isaiah 42:1-9

Spiritual Exercises 136-138

SPIRITUAL EXERCISES

I ask for the gift of being able to recognize the false lights of Lucifer . . . and for the help not to be led astray; I also ask for what I desire: a graced knowledge of true human living exemplified in Jesus Christ, my Lord and my God, and the grace to live my life in his way (Spiritual Exercises 139).

SCRIPTURE

Jesus, full of the Holy Spirit, returned from the Jordan and was led by the Spirit in the wilderness, where for forty days he was tempted by the devil. He ate nothing at all during those days, and when they were over, he was famished. The devil said to him, "If you are the Son of God, command this stone to become a loaf of bread." Jesus answered him, "It is written, 'One does not live by bread alone.'" Then the devil led him up and showed him in an instant all the kingdoms of the world. And the devil said to him, "To you I will give their glory and all this authority; for it has been given over to me, and I give it to anyone I please. If you, then, will worship me, it will all be yours." Jesus answered him, "It is written, 'Worship the Lord your God, and serve only him.'" Then the devil took him to Jerusalem, and placed him on the pinnacle of the temple, saying to him, "If you are the Son of God, throw yourself down from here, for it is written, 'He will command his angels concerning you, to protect you' . . . ." Jesus answered him, "It is said, 'Do not put the Lord your God to the test.'" When the devil had finished every test, he departed from him until an opportune time (Luke 4:1-13).

QUESTIONS

What gift or relationship do I hold in such importance that it becomes the "riches" for which I expect honor?

How do I experience being misunderstood or dismissed as one without importance?

Do I allow my experiences to be stepping stones to a more intimate following of Jesus? What image of Jesus can I use to counter my tendency to act as one who is entitled to power, prestige, and honor?

Have I developed a way of praying that includes asking Mary, the mother of Jesus, and Jesus for help in being a more faithful disciple?

How do the pressures of my culture, through all forms of media, lure me (sometimes unconsciously) into making decisions regarding what I purchase, wear, value, recommend?

What choices does the gospel call me to make regarding the increasing cultural diversity of our nation and my own environment?

What are the key temptations in my life and what happens within me when I allow myself to be controlled by them? What happens when, through grace, I resist?

AID TO DISCERNMENT

Light a candle during prayer as a symbolic reminder of your desire to live in God's light.

A time of consolation should provide the opportunity for a growth in true humility. . . . Acknowledge with gratitude the gifts we have received . . . take stock of how poorly we fare when such consolation is withdrawn. . . . If we are afflicted by desolation, we should take some consolation in knowing that God's grace is always sufficient to follow the way of the Lord (Spiritual Exercises 324).

The evil spirit often behaves like a spoiled child. If a person is firm with children, children give up petulant ways of acting. . . . So our tactics must include firmness in dealing with the evil spirit in our lives (Spiritual Exercises 325).

So does the evil spirit often act in a way to keep temptations secret, and our tactics must be to bring our temptations out into the light of day to someone like our director, confessor, or some other spiritual person (Spiritual Exercises 326).

The evil spirit . . . attacks at weak points. . . . Weakness is found in two ways: (a) the weakness of fragility or unpreparedness, and (b) the weakness of complacent strength which is self-sufficient pride (Spiritual Exercises 327).

EXAMEN PRAYER

In this prayer, give attention to possible small, ordinary ways that you resist incorporating the attitudes of Jesus into your daily choices.

MOMENT 20

DESIRE

To be free enough to make choices which are in harmony with God's will as it unfolds in my life.

FURTHER RESOURCES

2 Corinthians 13:11

Galatians 5:22-23

Matthew 10:17-22

Spiritual Exercises 149-157

SPIRITUAL EXERCISES

I ask Jesus our Lord that I might not be deaf to his call in my life and that I might be ready and willing to do what he wants (Spiritual Exercises 91).

This prayer period is devoted to a consideration of three types of persons. Each one of them has come to have quite a few possessions—not always acquired in the most honest way or with the best of motives. In general, each one is a good person who would like to serve God, even to the extent that if these possessions were to come in the way of being open to God's invitation, each type of person would like to be free of them (Spiritual Exercises 150, 151).

SCRIPTURE

As they were going along the road, someone said to him, "I will follow you wherever you go." And Jesus said to him, "Foxes have holes, and birds of the air have nests; but the Son of Man has nowhere to lay his head." To another he said, "Follow me." But he said, "Lord, first let me go and bury my father." But Jesus said to him, "Let the dead bury their own dead; but as for you, go and proclaim the kingdom of God" (Luke 9:57-62).

Then he said to them all, "If any want to become my followers, let them deny themselves and take up their cross daily and follow me. For those who want to save their life will lose it, and those who lose their life for my sake will save it. What does it profit them if they gain the whole world, but lose or forfeit themselves?" (Luke 9:23-25).

Someone told him, "Look, your mother and your brothers are standing outside, wanting to speak to you." But to the one who had told him this, Jesus replied, "Who is my mother, and who are my brothers?" And pointing to his disciples, he said, "Here are my mother and my brothers! For whoever does the will of my Father in heaven is my brother and sister and mother" (Matthew 12:47-50).

QUESTIONS

What is my desire to do God's will when it means setting aside or giving up my own cherished dream or plan?

What plans am I holding on to in my relationship with my spouse or children or friends or within my work situation?

How far am I willing to go in sacrificing my own satisfaction or pleasure in order to love as completely and as selflessly as Jesus did in laying down his life?

What is my desire to be given God's grace to live as Jesus did in fidelity to God's will?

Do I freely encourage others to follow their heart without trying to manipulate or control their decisions?

Am I aware of any fears that prevent me from moving forward in freedom?

What did Jesus do when afraid, and what can I learn from his pattern of behavior?

AID TO DISCERNMENT

Make choices of food and drink which reflect your desire to have your entire life humbly ordered to God.

When we are trying to follow the loving invitation of God in our life, we will find that the good spirit tends to give support, encouragement, and oftentimes even a certain delight in all our endeavors (Spiritual Exercises 329).

On the one hand, the good spirit brings about . . . consolation in order to strengthen and to speed the progress of our life in Christ. The evil spirit, on the other hand, arouses good feelings so that we might be drawn to focus our attention on wrong things, or to pursue a more selfish motivation, or to get our own way before all else. Quietly and slowly the change is brought about until the evil direction becomes set and clear (Spiritual Exercises 331).

SUGGESTION

Carry out your intention to do something about which you have been procrastinating.

EXAMEN PRAYER

When asking for God's light at the beginning of the Examen Prayer, ask for light concerning God's will in your life.

MOMENT 21

DESIRE

To grow in my ability to make good choices when faced with important decisions in my life.

SPIRITUAL EXERCISES

My life is firmly grounded in the fact that the reality of being a person is seen fully in Jesus Christ. "Just as I have come to do your will, O God" is the motivating force of his life, so the only real principle of choice in my life is to seek out and to do the will of God. . . . With this habitual attitude, I find that I can maintain a certain balance in my inclinations. . . . I would not want to turn away from God even in small ways, because my whole desire is to respond ever more faithfully to God's calls and invitations (Spiritual Exercises 166).

FURTHER RESOURCES

2 Corithians 13:5

Galatians 2:20

John 3:28-30

Ephesians 3:20-21

SCRIPTURE

In the morning, while it was still very dark, he got up and went out to a deserted place, and there he prayed. And Simon and his companions hunted for him. When they found him, they said to him, "Everyone is searching for you." He answered, "Let us go on to the neighboring towns, so that I may proclaim the message there also; for that is what I came out to do" (Mark 1:35-39).

"But the Advocate, the Holy Spirit, whom the Father will send in my name, will teach you everything, and remind you of all that I have said to you" (John 14:26).

"My grace is sufficient for you, for power is made perfect in weakness." So, I will boast all the more gladly of my weaknesses, so that the power of Christ may dwell in me. Therefore I am content with weaknesses, insults, hardships, persecutions, and calamities for the sake of Christ; for whenever I am weak, then I am strong (2 Corinthians 12:9-10).

. . . for I have learned to be content with whatever I have. I know what it is to have little, and I know what it is to have plenty. In any and all circumstances I have learned the secret of being well-fed and of going hungry, of having plenty and of being in need. I can do all things through him who strengthens me (Philippians 4:9, 11-13).

. . . for it is God who is at work in you, enabling you both to will and to work for his good pleasure (Philippians 2:13).

QUESTIONS

What do I need to do to be ready to make an important decision?

What can I do to provide the time, data, and reflection needed to make a good decision?

How do I check out my motivation as I move into decision-making?

What helps me to take into account rather than ignore the apparently conflicting pulls which I experience during decision-making?

What circumstances have brought me to the point of needing to make a decision?

What can I learn when I consider how my decision may affect others with whom I live or am close to?

AID TO DISCERNMENT

Notice the pendulum-like swing of your thoughts, feelings, and reflections as you are in a decision-making process.

Quite frequently we experience a time of alternating certainties and doubts, of exhilarating strength and debilitating weakness, of consolation and of desolation. As a matter of fact, this time is very privileged, because the discernment of spirits which is called for is an entrance into understanding a language of God spoken within our very being. We can gain much light and understanding from the experience of consolation and desolation, and so this time, too, is very special for decision making (Spiritual Exercises 176).

SUGGESTION

Make a list of the decisions you anticipate you will have to make in the next six months.

EXAMEN PRAYER

As you consider your daily responses, pay particular attention to the motivation within you as you made the response.

65

DESIRE

To appreciate the depth of faith and love which guided Jesus in his decisions.

FURTHER RESOURCES

Luke 21:37-38

Matthew 11:25-27

SPIRITUAL EXERCISES

I so much want the truth of Jesus' life to be fully the truth of my own that I find myself, moved by grace . . . [asking] to follow Jesus Christ in the most intimate union possible, that his experiences are reflected in my own. In that, I find my delight (Spiritual Exercises 167).

We may find it helpful at this time of the retreat when we might discover some attachment . . . or when we are not indifferent to poverty and riches, to come to Jesus our Lord in prayer and beg him to choose us to serve him. . . . We should beg with a certain insistence, and should plead for it—but always wanting what God wants for us (Spiritual Exercises 157).

SCRIPTURE

Then Jesus, filled with the power of the Spirit, returned to Galilee, and a report about him spread through all the surrounding country. He began to teach in their synagogues and was praised by everyone. When he came to Nazareth, where he had been brought up, he went to the synagogue on the sabbath day, as was his custom. He stood up to read, and the scroll of the prophet Isaiah was given to him. . . . "The Spirit of the Lord is upon me, because he has anointed me to bring good news to the poor. He has sent me to proclaim release to the captives and recovery of sight to the blind, to let the oppressed go free, to proclaim the year of the Lord's favor." . . . The eyes of all in the synagogue were fixed on him. Then he began to say to them, "Today this scripture has been fulfilled in your hearing" (Luke 4:14-21).

When the days draw near for him to be taken up, he set his face to go to Jerusalem (Luke 9:51).

From that time on, Jesus began to show his disciples that he must go to Jerusalem and undergo great suffering . . . and be killed, and on the third day be raised. And Peter took him aside and began to rebuke him, saying, "God forbid it, Lord! This must never happen to you." But he turned and said to Peter, "Get behind me, Satan! You are a stumbling block to me; for you are setting your mind not on divine things but on human things." Then Jesus told his disciples, "If any want to become my followers, let them deny themselves and take up their cross and follow me. For those who want to save their life will lose it, and those who lose their life for my sake will find it. For what will it profit them if they gain the whole world but forfeit their life? Or what will they give in return for their life?" (Matthew 16:21-26).

QUESTIONS

What are the "costs" to me of being a disciple of Jesus on a daily basis?

What forms of prayer help me at the time of a painful or important decision?

What have been the major decisions in my life?

What dimension is added to my experience when I recognize that God's will is basic to any significant decision I must make?

How do I celebrate when my decision has been the occasion of good in the lives of others?

When the burdens of decisions seem unbearable, particularly as they relate to my personal vocation, what can I learn from Jesus about laying down my life for others?

In taking a few moments to reflect on my style of decision-making (impulsive? procrastinator? collaborative?) and how it affects others, what might Jesus be trying to tell me?

AID TO DISCERNMENT

Look at earlier significant decisions in your life and notice the effect which they had upon your living out your personal call.

As we continue to make progress in the spiritual life, the movement of the good spirit is very delicate, gentle and often delightful. The good spirit touches us in the way that a drop of water penetrates a sponge. When the evil spirit tries to interrupt our progress, the movement is violent, disturbing, and confusing. The way that the evil spirit touches into our lives is more like water hitting hard upon a stone (Spiritual Exercises 335).

SUGGESTION

Ponder the faith and love which you saw at work in your parents' and grandparents' decisions.

EXAMEN PRAYER

When reviewing the day, consider the motivations you had in making decisions that will affect others.

REPLAYING THE MOMENTS III

People sometimes flee from a powerful moment of intimacy with God; the use of repetition gently holds us in God's presence. Given the pace of our busy lives, sometimes we are not well disposed as we come before God in prayer. Repetition allows us to become more and more open, attentive, and receptive to God's action. The prayer of repetition allows our feelings and emotions to be more fully expressed.

The following questions are meant to guide you in the repetition of Moments 11-22.

As you review the **Desires** of the past days or weeks, what desire continues to capture your attention and hold your interest? Take that desire to the Lord in prayer.

As you look back over this time period, what insight from *The Spiritual Exercises* surprised you with its practical wisdom? Ponder that insight and reflect on how you can incorporate that piece of wisdom into the rhythm of your life.

What **Scripture** passage continues to surface in your consciousness as you reflect on the word of God and your life? What is the Lord saying to you through that passage?

You have seen some practical **Suggestions** presented for your consideration. What suggestions did you find helpful? How are the suggestions helping you to integrate your prayer and ordinary life?

The **Questions** have focused on practical aspects of your life. How have you been helped or challenged by the questions?

During the past days or weeks, several **Aids to Discernment** have been suggested. Where did you find yourself to be most consoled? Prayerfully savor that consolation and allow the experience to deepen within you.

How has the **Examen Prayer** helped you to become more aware of God's presence and action in your life? Reflect on this awareness and allow the Lord to deepen it within your consciousness.

What captured your attention in the **Photograph**? How does the photograph support the desires, awarenesses, and insights within your experience of prayer during the last several Moments?

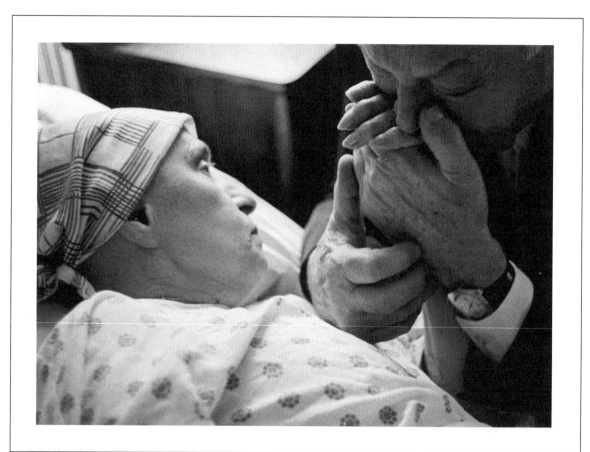

PRELUDE IV

"Do not weep for me,
but . . . for your children."

LUKE 23:28

The goodness and compassion of Jesus compels us to stay with him through the difficult days of his passion.

As teacher, Jesus gives us a final lesson about love, service, unity, humility, and remembrance.

Though powerless to prevent his human suffering, we learn from Mary how to stay faithful when one we love suffers even unto death.

Gradually we recognize in Jesus' suffering the love of God for sinners of every nation, as well as the meaning of human suffering.

Strengthened by Jesus' passion and death, we claim our hope in God's triumph over death, over suffering and sorrow of every kind.

We embrace the mission of Jesus "to bring good news to the poor. . . . to proclaim release to the captives and recovery of sight to the blind, to let the oppressed go free, to proclaim the year of the Lord's favor" (Luke 4:18-19).

Moment 23

"When You Do This, Remember Me"

Desire

To grow in my appreciation of the eucharist as Jesus' self-gift.

Spiritual Exercises

To enter as fully as I can into the preparations for the Passover meal . . . the Last Supper . . . goes beyond picturing the scene or reading the account in words. I try to listen to the ways words are spoken; I attempt to see the expression on the face; I am present with as heightened an awareness as I can muster, so that I enter as fully as possible into the mystery I am contemplating (Spiritual Exercises 191, 192, 194, 195-197).

Scripture

. . . the disciples did as Jesus had directed them, and they prepared the Passover meal. When it was evening, he took his place with the twelve. . . . While they were eating, Jesus took a loaf of bread, and after blessing it he broke it, gave it to the disciples, and said, "Take, eat; this is my body." Then he took a cup, and after giving thanks he gave it to them, saying, "Drink from it, all of you; for this is my blood of the covenant, which is poured out for many for the forgiveness of sins. I tell you, I will never again drink of this fruit of the vine until that day when I drink it new with you in my Father's kingdom" (Matthew 26:19, 20, 26-30).

For I received from the Lord what I also handed on to you, that the Lord Jesus on the night when he was betrayed took a loaf of bread, and when he had given thanks, he broke it and said, "This is my body that is for you. Do this in remembrance of me." In the same way he took the cup also, after supper, saying, "This cup is the new covenant in my blood. Do this, as often as you drink it, in remembrance of me." For as often as you eat this bread and drink the cup, you proclaim the Lord's death until he comes. Whoever, therefore, eats the bread or drinks the cup of the Lord in an unworthy manner will be answerable for the body and blood of the Lord. Examine yourselves, and only then eat of the bread and drink of the cup (1 Corinthians 11:23-29).

Further Resources

Isaiah 61:1-3, 6, 8-9

Exodus 12:1-8, 11-14

Psalm 116:12-13, 15-18

John 13:1-15

Mark 14:3-9

John 6:1-15

John 6:47-71

Revelation 1:5-8

QUESTIONS

What do I remember about my initial experiences of the eucharist? How have those experiences influenced the significance I give to the eucharist in my adult life?

How does being part of a community of believers help me to make the continued act of faith which the eucharist requires?

What have reverent moments of receiving the eucharist taught me about intimacy?

Have I made the connections between eucharist and service which are shown by Jesus at the Last Supper? Do I experience the eucharist as strengthening me to serve as Jesus did?

In what ways am I bread that is broken and shared with others on a daily basis?

AID TO DISCERNMENT

Notice the encouragement which the eucharistic prayers offer to you.

Spiritual Consolation . . . describes our interior life. . . . Such consolation often comes in a deep realization of ourselves as sinner before a loving and compassionate God, or in the face of Jesus' Passion when we see that Jesus loves and entrusts himself to God his Father and to us without limit . . . (Spiritual Exercises 316).

SUGGESTION

Talk with a young child or an elderly adult about the gift of the eucharist.

EXAMEN PRAYER

On Sunday, bring to your worship your awareness of the need for God's mercy which has grown in you by making the Examen Prayer through-out the week.

MOMENT 24

DESIRE

To learn from Mary's place in Jesus' life and death.

FURTHER RESOURCES

Isaiah 42:1-7

Psalm 31:2-6, 12-17

Luke 2:33-35

Luke 2:41-45

John 2:1-12

Luke 7:11-17

SPIRITUAL EXERCISES

I continue to pray for the gift of being able to feel sorrow with Jesus in sorrow, to be anguished with Jesus' anguish, and even to experience tears and deep grief because of all the afflictions which Jesus endures for me (Spiritual Exercises 203).

SCRIPTURE

Meanwhile, standing near the cross of Jesus were his mother, and his mother's sister, Mary the wife of Clopas, and Mary Magdalene. When Jesus saw his mother and the disciple whom he loved standing beside her, he said to his mother, "Woman, here is your son." Then he said to the disciple, "Here is your mother." And from that hour the disciple took her into his own home (John 19:25-27).

Blessed be the God and Father of our Lord Jesus Christ, the Father of mercies and the God of all consolation, who consoles us in all our affliction, so that we may be able to console those who are in any affliction with the consolation with which we ourselves are consoled by God. For just as the sufferings of Christ are abundant for us, so also our consolation is abundant through Christ. If we are being afflicted, it is for your consolation and salvation; if we are being consoled, it is for your consolation, which you experience when you patiently endure the same sufferings that we are also suffering. Our hope for you is unshaken; for we know that as you share in our sufferings, so also you share in our consolation (2 Corinthians 1:3-7).

QUESTIONS

When I reflect on my experience, what do I discover has contributed to my developing a relationship with Mary?

Have devotional prayers and artistic images helped or hindered my growth in a mature relationship with Mary?

Which qualities of Mary stand out for me in the scriptural stories which mention her?

When do I pray to Mary? What is significant for me about approaching the Mother of Jesus?

What does Mary's role in the life of Jesus teach me about compassion?

Mary knew how to integrate suffering into her faith response. What application does her example have for my life?

AID TO DISCERNMENT

Read Luke's account of the Annunciation (Luke 1:26-38) and ponder Mary's discernment of God's invitation to her.

When we are enjoying a consolation period, we should use foresight and savor the strength of such a period against the time when we may no longer find ourselves in consolation (Spiritual Exercises 323).

SUGGESTION

Recall and, if possible, view some of the many artistic presentations of Mary's place at the birth and death of Jesus.

EXAMEN PRAYER

As you become aware of your need of a particular grace in order to be more faithful to God's invitation, ask Mary to join you in asking God for that grace.

DESIRE

To experience sorrow and compassion for Jesus in his suffering.

FURTHER RESOURCES

Micah 6:1-8

Hebrews 4:14-16; 5:7-9

Philippians 2:4-11

Philippians 1:29

2 Timothy 1:8-12

Philippians 3:7-15

SPIRITUAL EXERCISES

The grace I seek is that God would gift me with a way of entering into sorrow and shame as I stay with Jesus in his sufferings borne on my behalf and because of my sins (Spiritual Exercises 193).

SCRIPTURE

When they had sung the hymn, they went out to the Mount of Olives. Then Jesus said to them, "You will all become deserters because of me this night; for it is written, 'I will strike the shepherd, and the sheep of the flock will be scattered.' But after I am raised up, I will go ahead of you to Galilee." Peter said to him, "Though all become deserters because of you, I will never desert you." Jesus said to him, "Truly I tell you, this very night, before the cock crows, you will deny me three times." Peter said to him, "Even though I must die with you, I will not deny you." And so said all the disciples. Then Jesus went with them to a place called Gethsemane; and he said to his disciples, "Sit here while I go over there and pray." He took with him Peter and the two sons of Zebedee, and began to be grieved and agitated. Then he said to them, "I am deeply grieved, even to death; remain here, and stay awake with me." And going a little farther, he threw himself on the ground and prayed, "My Father, if it is possible, let this cup pass from me; yet not what I want but what you want." Then he came to the disciples and found them sleeping; and he said to Peter, "So, could you not stay awake with me one hour? Stay awake and pray that you may not come into the time of trial; the spirit indeed is willing, but the flesh is weak." Again he went away for the second time and prayed, "My Father, if this cannot pass unless I drink it, your will be done." Again he came and found them sleeping, for their eyes were heavy. So leaving them again, he went away and prayed for the third time, saying the same words. Then he came to the disciples and said to them, "Are you still sleeping and taking your rest? See, the hour is at hand, and the Son of Man is betrayed into the hands of sinners" (Matthew 26:30-46).

QUESTIONS

What have I learned from my personal sorrows and sufferings?

What opportunities have I had to share in another's suffering? What have I learned from their personal sorrows and sufferings?

How does the narrative of Jesus' suffering and death help me to find meaning in what can appear to be the absurdity of suffering?

As a person of faith, how do I respond in faith to others who support positions different from my own?

When bad things happen to good people, how do I react to those who blame God for not interceding?

AID TO DISCERNMENT

Wordless presence with Jesus in times of sorrow and suffering can be a consoling experience.

Oftentimes in desolation, we feel that God has left us to fend for ourselves. By faith, we know that God is always with us in the strength and power of grace, but at the time of apparent abandonment we are little aware of God's continuing care and concern. We experience neither the support nor the sweetness of divine love, and our own response lacks fervor and intensity. It is as if we are living a skeletal life of the bare bones of faith (Spiritual Exercises 320).

SUGGESTION

Spend some time with people who are suffering. In addition to hospitals, nursing homes, and homeless shelters, you may find them in courtrooms, counseling centers, dining rooms, classrooms, finance meetings, cocktail parties, research labs, and your own home.

EXAMEN PRAYER

Be alert to how your attitude toward suffering contributes to your daily responses.

DESIRE

To deepen my faith in God's redeeming action in the midst of worldwide human suffering.

FURTHER RESOURCES

Isaiah 49:1-7

Isaiah 50:4-11

Isaiah 52:13–53:12

Matthew 9:35-38

Matthew 5:1-12

Luke 13:34-35

Romans 8:22-27

Romans 5:1-8

SPIRITUAL EXERCISES

I make even greater effort to labor with Jesus through all his pain, his struggle, his suffering, or what he is willing to suffer. At the time of the Passion, I should pay special attention to how the divinity hides itself so that Jesus seems so utterly human and helpless. I should make every effort to get inside the Passion, not just staying with external sufferings, but entering into the loneliness, the interior pain of rejection and feeling hated, all the anguish within Jesus. To realize that Jesus loves me so much that he willingly suffers everything for my rejections and my sins makes me ask: What response ought I make? (Spiritual Exercises 197).

SCRIPTURE

As they led him away, they seized a man, Simon of Cyrene . . . and they laid the cross on him, and made him carry it behind Jesus. A great number of the people followed him, and among them were women. . . . But Jesus turned to them and said, "Daughters of Jerusalem, do not weep for me, but weep for yourselves and for your children" (Luke 23:26-28).

Who will separate us from the love of Christ? Will hardship, or distress, or persecution, or famine, or nakedness, or peril, or sword? As it is written, "For your sake we are being killed all day long; we are accounted as sheep to be slaughtered." No, in all these things we are more than conquerors through him who loved us. For I am convinced that neither death, nor life, nor angels, nor rulers, nor things present, nor things to come, nor powers, nor height, nor depth, nor anything else in all creation, will be able to separate us from the love of God in Christ Jesus our Lord (Romans 8:31-39).

"'Lord, when was it that we saw you hungry and gave you food, or thirsty and gave you something to drink? And when was it that we saw you a stranger and welcomed you, or naked and gave you clothing? And when was it that we saw you sick or in prison and visited you?' And the king will answer them, 'Truly I tell you, just as you did it to one of the least of these who are members of my family, you did it to me'" (Matthew 25:37-45).

QUESTIONS

What helps me to be open to the mystery of suffering worldwide without succumbing to despair or inertia?

How do I give expression to my compassion for the suffering people of the world?

How has the suffering which I have experienced or witnessed intensified my commitment to the principles of justice in the economic, legal, heath-care, and educational systems?

Have I acted on my beliefs? How can I be an agent of change?

How can I use various forms of communication and technology to voice my support or opposition to important issues of justice and human rights?

Since my mind and heart can go places my feet and hands cannot, in what ways do I think globally when I pray?

AID TO DISCERNMENT

Notice any agitation which you experience when you are confronted by the suffering in the world.

Spiritual Desolation . . . describes our interior life: (a) when we find ourselves enmeshed in a certain turmoil of spirit or feel ourselves weighed down by a heavy darkness or weight; (b) when we experience a lack of faith or hope or love in the distaste for prayer or for any spiritual activity and we know a certain restlessness or tepidity in our carrying on in the service of God; (c) when we experience just the opposite effect of . . . spiritual consolation. For we will notice that the thoughts of rebelliousness, despair, or selfishness which arise at the time of desolation are in absolute contrast with the thoughts of the praise and service of God which flow during the time of consolation (Spiritual Exercises 317).

SUGGESTION

Recall the suffering you have become aware of recently whether in your neighborhood or in the nation or world.

EXAMEN PRAYER

As you pray in gratitude for the gifts of the day, include gratitude for your faith in the redeeming power of the life-death-resurrection of Jesus.

DESIRE

To allow experiences of powerlessness and waiting to prepare me for the gift of renewed faith in the resurrection.

FURTHER RESOURCES

Psalm 130:1-8

Sirach 11:20-21

Isaiah 54:5-14

Ezekiel 36:22-28

Romans 6:3-11

John 14:23-29

SPIRITUAL EXERCISES

When we find prayer dry and even a burden, we must be sure to spend the full hour as part of our attempt to respond by waiting for the Lord (Spiritual Exercises 13).

SCRIPTURE

Now there was a good and righteous man named Joseph, who, though a member of the council, had not agreed to their plan and action. . . . This man went to Pilate and asked for the body of Jesus. Then he took it down, wrapped it in a linen cloth, and laid it in a rock-hewn tomb where no one had ever been laid. It was the day of Preparation, and the sabbath was beginning. The women who had come with him from Galilee followed, and they saw the tomb and how his body was laid. Then they returned, and prepared spices and ointments. On the sabbath they rested according to the commandment (Luke 23:50-56).

I consider that the sufferings of this present time are not worth comparing with the glory about to be revealed to us. For the creation waits with eager longing for the revealing of the children of God; for the creation was subjected to futility, not of its own will but by the will of the one who subjected it, in hope that the creation itself will be set free from its bondage to decay and will obtain the freedom of the glory of the children of God. We know that the whole creation has been groaning in labor pains until now; and not only the creation, but we ourselves, who have the first fruits of the Spirit, groan inwardly while we wait for adoption, the redemption of our bodies. For in hope we were saved. Now hope that is seen is not hope. For who hopes for what is seen? But if we hope for what we do not see, we wait for it with patience (Romans 8:18-25).

Wait for the Lord; be strong, and let your heart take courage; wait for the Lord! (Psalm 27:14).

QUESTIONS

What do I do with feelings of loss and emptiness?

How do I face uncertainty, confusion, or anxiety?

What does being powerless in a situation lead me to do? How do I cope or respond?

What have I learned about the place of waiting or non-action in human life?

What are symbols of hope that offer me reassurance at times of discouragement or grieving? What or who is the source of my hope and strength?

In what ways have I shared my hope with another simply by being present to them and listening without trying to "fix"?

AID TO DISCERNMENT

Allow yourself to be aware of your need for hope in God's promise of fidelity to you and those you love.

God loves me so much, even entering into the very struggle of life. Like a potter with clay, like a mother in childbirth, or like a mighty force blowing life into dead bones, God labors to share divine life and love. God's labors are writ large in Jesus' passion and death on a cross in order to bring forth the life of the Resurrection (Spiritual Exercises 236).

SUGGESTION

Regardless of the season, walk around your garden or plants and observe the rhythm of life-death-new life at work there.

EXAMEN PRAYER

As you pray for God's help in the upcoming day, include an expression of your hope and confidence in God's power to change you.

REPLAYING THE MOMENTS IV

The use of the repetitions involves the whole person and emphasizes the importance of reflection on experience. Repetition is grounded in the wisdom of pondering in depth the reality and significance of our prayer experience. **Replaying the Moments** invites you to use the wisdom found in repetition as a way of reviewing and allowing God to deepen the awarenesses and gifts of a given portion of *Moment by Moment*.

The following questions will guide you in the repetition of Moments 23-27.

As you review the **Desires** of the past days or weeks, what desire continues to capture your attention and hold your interest? Take that desire to the Lord in prayer.

As you look back over this time period, what insight from *The Spiritual Exercises* surprised you with its practical wisdom? Ponder that insight and reflect on how you can incorporate that piece of wisdom into the rhythm of your life.

What **Scripture** passage continues to surface in your consciousness as you reflect on the word of God and your life? What is the Lord saying to you through that passage?

You have seen some practical **Suggestions** presented for your consideration. What suggestions did you find helpful? How are the suggestions helping you to integrate your prayer and ordinary life?

The **Questions** have focused on practical aspects of your life. How have you been helped or challenged by the questions?

During the past days or weeks, several **Aids to Discernment** have been suggested. Where did you find yourself to be most consoled? Prayerfully savor that consolation and allow the experience to deepen within you.

How has the **Examen Prayer** helped you to become more aware of God's presence and action in your life? Reflect on this awareness and allow the Lord to deepen it within your consciousness.

What captured your attention in the **Photograph**? How does the photograph support the desires, awarenesses, and insights within your experience of prayer during the last several Moments?

PRELUDE V

Thanks be to God for his indescribable gift!

2 CORINTHIANS 9:15

God raised Jesus from death to new life—to the astonishment of all but Mary, who had trusted completely the promise of the God to whom she had said "yes."

The gift of resurrection turns us around, makes us view everything differently, pokes at our residual doubt, fear, and attempts to control life.

We discover in the risen Christ a friend who consoles us and never leaves us, but continually invites us to new places in our life's journey.

Empowered by our experience of the risen Christ, we move as servants of Christ's mission into a world in need of transformation and change.

Grateful that "all is gift" and confident in God's power to save, we move on as servants—moment by moment.

DESIRE

To experience a deep joy in the fact of the resurrection of Jesus Christ.

SPIRITUAL EXERCISES

Jesus appeared first to the Virgin Mary. This, although it is not said in Scripture, is included in saying that he appeared to so many others . . . (Spiritual Exercises 299).

In the usual way, I try to enter into this contemplation as fully as I can. Although I do not have a Scripture account to guide my thoughts, I can easily know the excitement of Jesus in wanting to share the joy of his resurrection with his mother Mary who had stood by him throughout the passion. I let the delight and the love of this encounter permeate my being (Spiritual Exercises 219, 220, 222-224).

SCRIPTURE

FURTHER RESOURCES

1 Thessalonians 4:13-18

Matthew 28:1-10

Mark 16:1-8

Luke 24:1-12

Romans 14:7-9

Romans 6:3-11

Early on the first day of the week, while it was still dark, Mary Magdalene came to the tomb and saw that the stone had been removed from the tomb. . . . Mary stood weeping outside the tomb. As she wept, she bent over to look into the tomb; and she saw two angels in white, sitting where the body of Jesus had been lying, one at the head and the other at the feet. They said to her, "Woman, why are you weeping?" She said to them, "They have taken away my Lord, and I do not know where they have laid him." When she had said this, she turned around and saw Jesus standing there, but she did not know that it was Jesus. Jesus said to her, "Woman, why are you weeping? Whom are you looking for?" Supposing him to be the gardener, she said to him, "Sir, if you have carried him away, tell me where you have laid him, and I will take him away." Jesus said to her, "Mary! . . . Do not hold on to me, because I have not yet ascended to the Father. . . ." Mary Magdalene went and announced to the disciples, "I have seen the Lord"; and she told them that he had said these things to her (John 20:1-18).

Then I saw a new heaven and a new earth; for the first heaven and the first earth had passed away. . . . And I saw the holy city, the new Jerusalem, coming down out of heaven from God, prepared as a bride adorned for her husband. And I heard a loud voice from the throne saying, "See, the home of God is among mortals. He will dwell with them as their God; they will be his peoples, and God himself will be with them; he will wipe every tear from their eyes. Death will be no more; mourning and crying and pain will be no more. . . . See, I am making all things new." Also he said, "Write this, for these words are trustworthy and true." Then he said to me, "It is done! I am the Alpha and the Omega, the beginning and the end. To the thirsty I will give water as a gift from the spring of the water of life" (Revelation 21:1-7).

QUESTIONS

In what areas of my life and relationships am I now experiencing new life after a time of struggle and loss? Do I allow myself to be surprised? Do I surprise others in loving ways?

What new configurations of thought, attitude, and action seem required in my life as a result of my faith in the risen Christ?

Is my faith and hope in the risen Christ the foundation of my peace and happiness even though my life continues to have struggle and suffering as part of it?

If I take a few minutes to reflect on (or be with) Mary as she encounters the risen Lord, what words burst forth from me at such a graced moment?

How does my faith and hope in the resurrection help me to be more compassionate and understanding of the struggles of people within the church?

AID TO DISCERNMENT

Notice the quiet attentiveness to God's presence and action which has grown within you.

When we are enjoying a consolation period, we should use foresight and savor the strength of such a period against the time when we may no longer find ourselves in consolation (Spiritual Exercises 323).

In [this] week, I make some modifications . . . toward making the whole day consistently prayerful.
    As soon as I awake, I recall the atmosphere of joy which pervades this week and review the particular mystery about which I am to contemplate (Spiritual Exercises 229).

SUGGESTION

Listen to Handel's *Messiah* or to a contemporary song which conveys the theme of new life to you.

EXAMEN PRAYER

Pay attention to the presence of both joy and compassion as they mingle in your responses to people.

DESIRE

To encounter Christ as one who consoles me in my sadness and discouragement.

FURTHER RESOURCES

Acts 10:34-43

1 Peter 1:17-21

1 Corinthians 15:3-7, 12-14, 19-22

2 Corinthians 5:14-19

Isaiah 65:17-25

SPIRITUAL EXERCISES

. . . consider the role of consoling which Christ our Lord bears, and . . . consider how friends are accustomed to console friends (Spiritual Exercises 224).

SCRIPTURE

Now . . . two of them were going to . . . Emmaus . . . and talking with each other about all these things that had happened. While they were talking and discussing, Jesus himself came near and went with them, but their eyes were kept from recognizing him. And he said to them, "What are you discussing with each other while you walk along?" They stood still, looking sad. "Are you the only stranger in Jerusalem who does not know the things that have taken place there . . . ?" He asked them, "What things?" They replied, "The things about Jesus of Nazareth, who was a prophet mighty in deed and word before God and all the people, and how our chief priests and leaders handed him over to be condemned to death and crucified him. But we had hoped that he was the one to redeem Israel. . . . Moreover, some women of our group astounded us. . . . When they did not find his body [at the tomb], they came back and told us that they had indeed seen a vision of angels who said that he was alive. Some of those who were with us went to the tomb and found it just as the women had said; but they did not see him." Then he said to them, "Oh, how foolish you are, and how slow of heart to believe all that the prophets have declared! Was it not necessary that the Messiah should suffer these things and then enter into his glory?" Then beginning with Moses and all the prophets, he interpreted to them the things about himself in all the scriptures. As they came near the village to which they were going, he walked ahead as if he were going on. But they urged him strongly, saying, "Stay with us, because it is almost evening and the day is now nearly over." So he went in to stay with them. When he was at the table with them, he took bread, blessed and broke it, and gave it to them. Then their eyes were opened, and they recognized him; and he vanished from their sight. They said to each other, "Were not our hearts burning within us while he was talking to us on the road, while he was opening the scriptures to us?" That same hour they got up and returned to Jerusalem; and they found the eleven and their companions gathered together. They were saying, "The Lord has risen indeed, and he has appeared to Simon!" Then they told what had happened on the road, and how he had been made known to them in the breaking of the bread (Luke 24:13-35).

QUESTIONS

What disappointments or hurts or failures are preventing me from moving on with my life? Would viewing them as a share in the death-resurrection of Jesus give me the freedom to entrust them to God?

Do I relate my eventual death with the resurrection of Jesus?

How often do I make time to "be there" for a family member, colleague, or neighbor?

What are comforting or consoling activities for me? Do I allow myself to enjoy them?

When have I been part of a project or effort in which I could sense my heart "burning within" from God's presence?

We walk through life's struggles and joys, not alone, but with other people. Who are my mentors in times of consolation and desolation? To what extent have I continued this blessing by quietly being a mentor for others?

Does the Lord's presence in my life cause my heart to "burn within" me as the disciples experienced on the way to Emmaus? Where do I direct this passion?

AID TO DISCERNMENT

Notice the signs within you which alert you to the fact that God is present to you.

Throughout the day, I try to keep myself in a mood which is marked by happiness and spiritual joy. As a result, anything in my environment—the sun and warm weather or the white cover of snow, all the different beauties of nature and so on—is used to reinforce the atmosphere of consolation (Spiritual Exercises 229).

SUGGESTION

Telephone or send an encouraging note or e-mail to a friend who has been having a hard time recently.

EXAMEN PRAYER

Pray in gratitude for the people who have been consolers to you in your life.

89

MOMENT 30

DESIRE

To deepen my faith and hope in the promises and power of the risen Christ.

FURTHER RESOURCES

Colossians 3:1-4

1 Peter 1:3-9

Psalm 118:21-29

Joel 2:23-28

1 Corinthians 15:51-58

SPIRITUAL EXERCISES

I beg for the grace of being able to enter into the joy and consolation of Jesus as he savors the victory of his risen life (Spiritual Exercises 221).

SCRIPTURE

When it was evening on that day, the first day of the week, and the doors of the house where the disciples had met were locked for fear of the Jews, Jesus came and stood among them and said, "Peace be with you." After he said this, he showed them his hands and his side. Then the disciples rejoiced when they saw the Lord. Jesus said to them again, "Peace be with you. As the Father has sent me, so I send you." When he had said this, he breathed on them and said to them, "Receive the Holy Spirit. If you forgive the sins of any, they are forgiven them; if you retain the sins of any, they are retained." But Thomas (who was called the Twin), one of the twelve, was not with them when Jesus came. So the other disciples told him, "We have seen the Lord." But he said to them, "Unless I see the mark of the nails in his hands, and put my finger in the mark of the nails and my hand in his side, I will not believe." A week later his disciples were again in the house, and Thomas was with them. Although the doors were shut, Jesus came and stood among them and said, "Peace be with you." Then he said to Thomas, "Put your finger here and see my hands. Reach out your hand and put it in my side. Do not doubt but believe." Thomas answered him, "My Lord and my God!" Jesus said to him, "Have you believed because you have seen me? Blessed are those who have not seen and yet have come to believe." Now Jesus did many other signs in the presence of his disciples, which are not written in this book. But these are written so that you may come to believe that Jesus is the Messiah, the Son of God, and that through believing you may have life in his name (John 20:19-31).

Always be ready to make your defense to anyone who demands from you an accounting for the hope that is in you (1 Peter 3:15).

QUESTIONS

How has my faith grown into a more personal relationship with God?

What continues to be the riskiest part of faith and hope for me?

To what or to whom do I turn to remain secure at times of change, uncertainty, and doubt?

What events in my life have been the occasions of developing a greater confidence in God's care for the world?

How have I experienced God's peace and promise of faithful presence through a friendship in my life?

AID TO DISCERNMENT

Read Lamentations 3:21-26.

God's love shines down upon me like the light rays from the sun, or God's love is poured forth lavishly like a fountain spilling forth its waters into an unending stream. Just as I see the sun in its rays and the fountain in its waters, so God pours forth a sharing in divine life in all the gifts showered upon me. God's delight and joy is to be with the ones called God's children—to be with me. God cannot do enough to speak out and show love for me—ever calling and inviting me to a fuller and better life, a sharing in divine life (Spiritual Exercises 237).

SUGGESTION

Take advantage of an opportunity to give verbal expression to your Christian faith.

EXAMEN PRAYER

Allow your prayer for God's help to reflect your hope in God's fidelity to you.

DESIRE

To draw upon my awareness of Christ's abiding presence to me as I reach out to others.

FURTHER RESOURCES

1 Corinthians 5:6-8

Acts 2:42-47

Acts 4:32-35

Acts 5:12-16

Acts 4:8-12

John 15:9-17

1 John 4:11-16

Ephesians 4:1-3

SPIRITUAL EXERCISES

. . . note how much the divinity shines through the person of Jesus in all his appearances. The peace and the joy which he wants to share with me can only be a gift of God. . . . the role of consoler which Jesus performs in each of his resurrection appearances is the same role he performs now: [this] . . . is a faith insight into why I can live my life in a true Christian optimism (Spiritual Exercises 224).

SCRIPTURE

Simon Peter said to them, "I am going fishing." They said to him, "We will go with you." They went out and got into the boat, but that night they caught nothing. Just after daybreak, Jesus stood on the beach; but the disciples did not know that it was Jesus. Jesus said to them, ". . . you have no fish, have you?" They answered him, "No." He said to them, "Cast the net to the right side of the boat, and you will find some." So they cast it, and now they were not able to haul it in because there were so many fish. That disciple whom Jesus loved said to Peter, "It is the Lord!" When Simon Peter heard that it was the Lord, he put on some clothes, for he was naked, and jumped into the sea. But the other disciples came in the boat, dragging the net full of fish . . . (John 21:1-8).

When they had gone ashore, they saw a charcoal fire there, with fish on it, and bread. Jesus said to them, "Bring some of the fish that you have just caught." So Simon Peter went aboard and hauled the net ashore, full of large fish, a hundred fifty-three of them; and though there were so many, the net was not torn. Jesus said to them, "Come and have breakfast." Now none of the disciples dared to ask him, "Who are you?" because they knew it was the Lord. Jesus came and took the bread and gave it to them, and did the same with the fish. This was now the third time that Jesus appeared to the disciples after he was raised from the dead (John 21:9-14).

QUESTIONS

What have I discovered about the way in which God's gifts are given to me and to others?

How does confidence in God's presence and action free me to take courageous steps?

How does it feel to know that I will be empowered by God to carry out my personal vocation?

How do I image my role as a follower of Christ in contemporary society?

With whom do I long to share my faith in Christ?

Being a man or woman for others involves gospel-based leadership. In what ways do I live this out by being a voice for the voiceless in my home, community, or workplace, especially concerning human rights and social justice issues?

AID TO DISCERNMENT

Notice the strengthening effect which faith in God has upon your self-confidence when facing challenges.

God . . . gifts me with the fullness of divine life in Jesus. God's only Son is not only the Word in whom all things are created, but also the Word who becomes flesh and dwells with us. . . . God loves me so much that I become a dwelling-place or temple of God—growing in an ever-deepening realization of the image and likeness of God which is the glory shining out of human creation (Spiritual Exercises 235).

SUGGESTION

Invite a friend to join you for breakfast, brunch, coffee, or tea.

EXAMEN PRAYER

Ask the Spirit to show you the opportunities you have to express your faith in daily surroundings.

DESIRE

To be so grateful for the gifts I have received that I will want to share them in service.

SPIRITUAL EXERCISES

I beg for the gift of an intimate knowledge of all the goods which God lovingly shares with me. Filled with gratitude, I want to be empowered to respond just as totally in my love and service (Spiritual Exercises 233).

SCRIPTURE

When they had finished breakfast, Jesus said to Simon Peter, "Simon son of John, do you love me more than these?" He said to him, "Yes, Lord; you know that I love you." Jesus said to him, "Feed my lambs." A second time he said to him, "Simon son of John, do you love me?" He said to him, "Yes, Lord; you know that I love you." Jesus said to him, "Tend my sheep." He said to him the third time, "Simon son of John, do you love me?" Peter felt hurt because he said to him the third time, "Do you love me?" And he said to him, "Lord, you know everything; you know that I love you." Jesus said to him, "Feed my sheep. Very truly, I tell you, when you were younger, you used to fasten your own belt and to go wherever you wished. But when you grow old, you will stretch out your hands, and someone else will fasten a belt around you and take you where you do not wish to go." (He said this to indicate the kind of death by which he would glorify God.) After this he said to him, "Follow me . . ." (John 21:15-19).

FURTHER RESOURCES

Ephesians 4:7, 11-16

Ephesians 1:17-23

Ephesians 3:9-21

1 Corinthians 13:1-13

Revelation 21:1-5

John 14:18, 25-26

QUESTIONS

What do I want to do to remain open to God's continuing faithful love for me?

What has become clearer to me about my relationship to God as it is expressed in my relationship to myself, my family, my colleagues, and the nation, world, and church of which I am a part?

How can I re-order my daily routine so that I stay both grounded in the truth of who I am and focused on serving God and God's people?

As I have grown in awareness and appreciation of God's goodness to me, Moment by Moment, in what practical ways will I continue to stay focused on Jesus as the ground of my being?

AID TO DISCERNMENT

Savor your growing awareness that all is gift from God.

Take, Lord, and receive all my liberty, my memory, my understanding, and my entire will—all that I have and call my own. You have given it all to me. To you, Lord, I return it. Everything is yours; do with it what you will. Give me only your love and grace. That is enough for me ("Take and Receive," Spiritual Exercises 234).

SUGGESTION

Plan a celebration of God's goodness for any who have shared in *Moment by Moment* with you.

EXAMEN PRAYER

Ask God's Spirit to lead you through the steps of the Examen Prayer.

GATHERING THE GRACED MOMENTS

In light of the **Desires** which you experienced in Moment by Moment, what has God been revealing to you in your desires? Take those desires and experiences to the Lord in prayer.

As you look back over the past days and weeks, what insight from *The Spiritual Exercises* surprised you with its practical wisdom? Ponder that insight and reflect on how you can incorporate that piece of wisdom into the rhythm of your life.

What **Scripture** passages have become important to you? What is the Lord saying to you in those passages?

You have seen some practical **Suggestions** presented in *Moment by Moment*. What have you learned from them about connecting faith and daily life?

The **Questions** have focused on your life. What questions do you want to continue to ponder? What questions are leading you to further action?

Aids to Discernment have been suggested. What have the aids to discernment taught you about being more discerning? What helps you to recognize when you are in consolation or desolation?

How has the **Examen Prayer** helped you to become more aware of God's presence and action in your life? Reflect on this awareness and allow the Lord to deepen it within your consciousness.

How has your prayer been affected by the **Photographs**? What change of attitude have they occasioned?

. . . love ought to show itself in deeds . . . love consists in a mutual sharing of goods (Spiritual Exercises 230-231).